OH YES! I CAN

OH YES! I CAN

2 Corinthians 5:17 "Therefore if any man be in Christ he is a new creature old things are passed away; behold all things are become new."

Thea A. Barnes

authorHOUSE®

AuthorHouse™
1663 Liberty Drive
Bloomington, IN 47403
www.authorhouse.com
Phone: 1-800-839-8640

First published by AuthorHouse   11/22/2011

ISBN: 978-1-4685-0562-7 (sc)
ISBN: 978-1-4685-0561-0 (ebk)

Library of Congress Control Number: 2011961021

Printed in the United States of America

YES, I CAN

I dedicate this book to Christine Dodd my beloved mother, Who has always been there for me, to my children, to my sister Linda Johnson who start me reading the Bible because one day I saw Linda reading the word of God and most of all I dedicate this book to the Lord Jesus Christ. He is my friend, My Lord, the head of my Life and I love him very much.

INTRODUCTION

The purpose of this book is to help bring the church back to the basic. We need more teaching on repent, water baptize, being fill with the Holy Ghost, and what it take to live a holy life. Thank the Lord for teaching on prosperity for we need it, I need it, especially in time like these. I just feel the church need more teaching on the basic. I believe in order to really get bless financially you must put the Lord first in your life. You need to seek first the kingdom of God and all of His righteousness and all the other things will be add to you.

I believe the church need to concentrate on living a holy life and teach young saint how to repent, and present their body as a living sacrifice, holy acceptable unto the Lord, which is our reasonable service. The Bible say the good work God has begun within us He will perform it until the day of the Lord Jesus Christ. I want the church to know what it take to Live holy.

I want saint to know what it real takes to live holy and grow in the knowledge of our Lord Jesus Christ. 2 Peter 1:2-12 Grace and peace be multiplied unto you through the knowledge of God, and of Jesus our Lord, According as His divine power hath given unto us all things that pertain unto life and godliness, through the knowledge of Him that hath called us to glory and virtue: Whereby are given unto us exceeding great and precious promises: that by these ye might be partakers of the divine nature, having escaped the corruption that is in the world through lust. And beside this, giving all diligence, add to your faith virtue; and to virtue knowledge; and to knowledge temperance; and to temperance patience; and to patience godliness; and to godliness brotherly kindness; and to brotherly kindness charity. For if these thing be in you, and abound, they make you that ye shall neither be barren nor unfruitful in the knowledge of our Lord Jesus Christ. But he that lacketh these things is blind, and cannot see afar off, and hath forgotten that he was purged from his old sins. Wherefore the rather, brethren, give diligence to make your calling and election sure: for if ye do these things, ye shall never fall: For so an entrance shall be ministered unto you abundantly into the everlasting kingdom of our Lord and Saviour Jesus Christ. Wherefore I will not be negligent to put you always in remembrance of these things, thought ye know them, and be established in the present truth.

I just want to help anyone who is having problem put their feet on the solid ground and living holy.

CONTENTS

The Bible say in ST. John 3:16 For God so loved the world, that He gave His only begotten son, that whosoever believeth in Him should not perish, but have everlasting life. Jesus demonstrated His love for you and me by dying on the cross. The Bible says greater love has no man than this that a man lay down his life for his friend. Jesus lay down his life for you. The love Jesus has for us is immeasurable. The greatest demonstration of God love is when Jesus dies on Calvary. Because Jesus loves us so much until He lay down His life for us we should so love our brother until we are willing to lay down our life for the brother.

Yes, I am love and therefore I can love. Deuteronomy 7:7-10 The Lord did not set His love upon you, nor choose you, because ye were more in number than any people; for ye were the fewest of all people: But because the Lord loved you and because He would keep the oath which He had sworn unto your fathers, hath the Lord brought you with a mighty hand, and redeemed you out of the house of bondmen, from the hand of Pharaoh King of Egypt. Know therefore that the Lord thy God, He is God, the faithful God, which keepeth covenant and mercy with them that love Him and keep His commandments to a thousand generations; And repayeth them that hate Him to their face to destroy them; He will not be slack to Him that hateth Him;, He will repay him to his face. God loves us therefore He will keep the promises that He have made to us. His love is not basis on circumstance, or on who we are or how large or small we are he just loves us and that love was shown on Calvary. Therefore because we have received His love therefore we can give love. Romans 5:1-5 Therefore being justified by faith, we have peace with God through our Lord Jesus Christ. By whom also we have access by faith into this grace wherein we stand, and rejoice in hope of the glory of God. And not only so, but we glory in tribulations also: knowing that tribulations worked patience; and patience, experience; and experience, hope; And hope maketh not ashamed; because the love of God is shed abroad in our hearts by the Holy Ghost which is give unto us. We can love other because His love is shed abroad in our heart by the Holy Ghost. We can love our spouse our husband and we can love our wives, children and friends because of Him.

Husband the Bible teaches the husband to love his wife as his own body. Ephesians 5:25-28 Husbands, love your wives, even as Christ also loved the church, and gave Himself for it; That He might sanctify and cleanse it with the washing of water by the word. That He might present it to Himself a glorious church, not having spot, or wrinkle, or any such thing; but that it should be Holy and without blemish. So ought men to love their wives as their own bodies. He that loveth his wife loveth himself. When a man loves his wife as Christ love the church, he teaches her to love him by example. You can love and be love because of the Lord Jesus Christ has loved you. Titus 2:1-5 But speak thou the things which become sound doctrine: That the aged men be sober, grave, temperate, sound in faith, in charity, in patience, The aged women likewise, that they be in behavior as becometh holiness, not false accusers, not given to much wine, teachers of good things; That they may teach the young women to be sober, to love their husbands, to love their children, To be discreet, chaste, keepers at home, good obedient to their own husbands, that the word of God be not blasphemed. When love is in the home patient is there, kindness is there and joy and peace will be there in the home.

I John 2:15 Love not the world, neither the things that are in the world. If any man loves the world, the love of the Father is not in him. We are instructed not to love the world, but what John is talking about is the world system the spirit is that of antichrist. John is not talking about the people of the world. John is talking about don't love the things of the world but we are to love the Lord with all our heart, mind, soul and strength. In St. John 3:16 The Bible is talking about people. For God so loved the world, that he gave his only begotten Son, that whosoever believeth in Him should not perish, but have everlasting life. Matthew 5:43-48 Ye have heard that it hath been said; Thou shalt love thy neighbor, and hate thine enemy. But I say unto you, Love your enemies, bless them that curse you, do good to them that hate you, and pray for them which despitefully use you, and persecute you; That you may be the children of your Father which is in heaven: for He maketh His sun to rise on the evil and on the good, and sendeth rain on the just and on the unjust. For if ye love them which love you, what reward have ye? Do not even the publicans the same? And if ye salute your brethren only, what do ye more than others? Do not even the publicans so? Be ye therefore perfect, even as your Father which is in heaven is perfect.

Phileo is one of the Greek words for love in the New Testament, which expresses a love of intimate affection, a love which receives personal pleasure in return. It loves because of what is received in return. The love of God is not basis on what can be return. God love is expressed by the Greek word agape. The highest form of love. Agape mean love because it is love which is God. Agape is a self-sacrificial love. It gives and surrenders without the thought of receiving anything in return. The Bible says in Romans 5:8-9 But God commendeth His love toward us, in that while we were yet sinners, Christ died for us. I John 3:16 Hereby perceive we the love of God, because he laid down His life for us, and we ought to lay down our lives for the brethren. But whoso hath this world's good, and seeth his brother have need, and shuttled up his bowels of compassion how dwelleth the love of God in him. Real love gives and gives.

Agape love caused Jesus to die on Calvary for our sin. John 15:13 Greater love hath no man than this that a man lay down his life for his friends. If a person lay down his life for you, there is no greater love than to lay down your life for another. This is what Jesus did for us?

Jeremiah said that God love for Israel was everlasting. Jeremiah 31:3 The Lord hath appeared of old unto me, saying, Yea I have loved thee with an everlasting love; therefore with lovingkindness have I drawn thee. God love for Israel is eternal both now and forever, and we are spiritual Jew.

The church has always been and will continue to be the object of God love. Romans 5:6 For when we were yet without strength, in due time Christ died for the ungodly. The church is filling with the love of God. Ephesians 1:22-23 And hath put all things under His feet, and gave Him to be the head over all things to the church, which is his body, the fullness of Him that filleth all in all. The body of Christ is filling with the Holy Ghost and is filling with the love of God.

The love of God in our heart said that we are saved that we belong to Jesus. I John 4:7-12 Beloved, let us love one another; for love is of God; and every one that loveth is born of God, and knoweth God. He that loveth not knoweth not God; for God is love. In this was manifested the love of God toward us, because that God sent His only begotten Son into the world, that we might live through Him. Herein is love, not that we loved God, but that He loved us, and sent His Son to be the propitiation for our sins, Beloved, if God so loved us, we ought also to love one another. No man hath seen God at any time, if we love one another, God dwelled in us, and His love is perfected in us.

As children of God, we are known by the fact that we have loved one for another. John 13:34-35 A new commandment I give unto you, that ye love one another; as I have loved you, that ye also love another. By this shall all men know that ye are my disciples, if ye have loved one to another? It is very important that God's children walk in love but the love that Jesus put within us is not just natural love. It is divine love that comes from the Lord. We get this love through the Holy Ghost. It is impossible to have agape love accept through the Holy Ghost.

God's love is without condition. He loves us no matter what if we are black, white, there is no prejudice and bigotry with God. If we sin He still loves us and is willing to forgive us, because that what love does it forgive and God is love. God love us while we were yet sinners. Romans 5:8 For God commendeth His love toward us, in that, while we were yet sinners, Christ died for us. He loved you and me before we even thought about loving Him. I John 4:10 Herein is love, not that we loved God, but that He loved us, and sent His Son to be the propitiation for our sins.

God's love there is no limit. Agape love is never exhausted. When we do wrong God still love us. When the prodigal son left home and waste his good his father never stop loving him. For he welcome him with open arms when he return home. Put a robe on him, shoes on his feet and a ring on his finger. Agape love never dies, nothing can quench it.

I Corinthians 13:1-8 Though I speak with the tongues of men and of angels, and have not charity, I am become as sounding brass, or a tinkling cymbal. And though I have the gift of prophecy, and understand all l mysteries, and all knowledge; and though I have all faith, so that I could remove mountains, and have not charity; I am nothing. And though I bestow all my goods to feed the poor, and though I give my body to be burned, and have not charity, it profited me nothing. Charity suffereth long, and is kind; charity envieth not; charity vaunteth not itself, is not puffed up. Doth not behave itself unseemly, seeketh not her own, is not easily provoked, thinketh no evil; rejoiceth not in iniquity, but rejoiceth in the truth; Beareth all things, believeth all things, hopeth all things, endureth all things. Charity never faileth.

Yes! I can love. And receive the love of God. For it is His love that dwelled within me. It is all because of Jesus that I can love and receive the love of God. I John 4:8 He that loveth not knoweth not God; for God is love. God love is measureless and reaches above all human limitations. We can express and describe the love of God if God live in us.

We are taught in the book of I John not to love the world. This is not speaking of the people of the world but the system of the world the things of the world we are not to love. I John 2:15 Love not the world, neither the things that are in the world. If any man loves the world, the love of the Father is not in Him. John is talk about the world system whose spirit is that of the antichrist. I John 5:19 And we know that we are of God, and the whole world lie in wickedness.

True love gives and is sacrifice. God has shown His love toward us by giving Himself for us and we show our love by serving Him and witnessing to the lost and by loving each other. Jesus is the greatest example of what love is. He came not into the world seeking fame or reputation. Philippians 2:5

Let this mind be in you, which was also in Christ Jesus. Who, being in the form of God, thought it not robbery to be equal with God: But made Himself of no reputation, and took upon Him the form of a servant, and was made in the likeness of men: And being found in fashion as a man, He humbled Himself, and became obedient unto death, even the death of the cross. He gave Himself for you and me.

God has command that you and I love one another. John 15: 12-13 This is my commandment, that ye love one another, as I have love you. Greater love has no man than this that a man lay down his life for his friends. The Bible say by this all men shall know that you are my disciple because you have loved one for another. We can love because the love of God is shed abroad in our heart by the Holy Ghost. Yes, we can love and receive love because of Jesus.

YES, I CAN HAVE FAITH. Hebrews 11:1 Now Faith the substance of things hoped for, the evidence of things of things not seen. Faith is not what you and I see it is what we believe in through the word of God. Hebrews 11:6 But without faith it is impossible to please Him: for he that cometh to God must believe that He is, and that He is a rewarded of them that diligently seek Him. The Lord has not asked us to do something that is impossible, the Bible says that God has dealt to every man the measure of faith. What you and I do with that faith is left up to us? We can let our faith grow or we can allow it to die, but God give every man a measure of faith.

Romans 10:17 says, So then faith cometh by hearing, and hearing by the word of God. We get faith through the word of God. I Corinthians 1:21 It pleased God by the foolishness of preaching to save them that believe.

13

Romans 10:12-15 For there is no difference between the Jew and the Greek; for the same Lord over all is rich unto all that call upon him. For whosoever shall call upon the name of the Lord shall be saved. How then shall they call on Him in whom they have not believed? And how shall they believe in Him of whom they have not heard? And how shall they hear without a preacher? And how shall they preach, except they are sent? As it is written, how beautiful are the feet of them that preach the gospel of peace, and bring glad tidings of good things!

We believe in God with our heart Romans 10:8-11 But what saith it? The word is nigh thee, even in thy mouth, and in thy heart: that is, the word of faith, which we preach; That if thou shall confess with thy mouth the Lord Jesus, and shall believe in thine heart that God hath raised Him from the dead, thou shall be saved. For with the heart man believeth unto righteousness; and with the mouth confession is made unto salvation. For the scripture saith, whosoever believeth on Him shall not be ashamed.

Everything we get from God come to us by faith. We get salvation, righteousness, sanctification, justification, direction; healing, pleasing God, victory, understanding, and wisdom all come to us by faith.

SALVATION: Unbelief will stop you and I from receiving our salvation form the Lord for which He paid a great price His life. Mark 1: 15 Repent ye, and believe the gospel. Ephesians 2:8-9 For by grace are ye saved through faith; and that not of yourselves: it is the gift of God. Not of works, lest any man should boast. John 7:37-39 In the last day, that great day of the feast, Jesus stood and cried, saying. If any man thirsts, let him come unto me, and drink. He that believeth on me, as the scripture hath said, out of his belly shall flow rivers of living water. (But this spake

He of the Spirit, which they that believe on Him should receive: for the Holy Ghost was not yet given; because that Jesus was not yet glorified.) Salvation comes to us through faith in the Lord Jesus Christ.

RIGHTEOUSNESS: Isaiah 64:6 But we are all as an unclean thing, and all our righteousneses are as filthy rags; and we all do fade as a leaf; and our iniquities, like the wind have taken us away. When we put on our righteousness we stink in the nostril of God. Romans 10:3 For they being ignorant of God righteousness, and going about to establish their own righteousness, have not submitted themselves unto the righteousness of God. For the righteousness of God is by faith we believe in the work He did on Calvary. Romans 9:30 What shall we say then? That the Gentiles, which followed not after righteousness, have attained to righteousness, even the righteousness which is of faith. If we want to attain righteousness through the law, we must remember if we break one law we are guilt of them all.

SANCTIFICATION: We get sanctification initially when we are born again but through faith we must retain and grow in the state of purification, holiness, and consecration. This occurs as we read and study the word of God. Acts 26:18 To open their eyes, and to turn them from darkness to light, and from the power of Satan unto God, that they may receive forgiveness of sins, and inheritance among them which are sanctified by faith that is in me.

JUSTIFICATION: Justification is being declared just, innocent, and righteous in the sight of God. Romans 5:1 Therefore being justified by faith, we have peace with God through our Lord Jesus Christ. Galatians 2:16 Knowing that a man is not justified by the works of the law, but by the faith of Jesus Christ. Galatians 3:24 Wherefore the law was our schoolmaster to bring us unto Christ, that we might be justified by faith. Romans 3:28 Therefore we conclude that a man is justified by faith without the deeds of the law. Thank God for faith.

DIRECTION: We all need direction in life which way to go, what question to ask we need direction. Psalm 27:11 Teach me thy way, O Lord, and lead me in a plain path, because of mine enemies. 2 Corinthians 5:7 For we walk by faith, not by sight. St. John 16:13 Howbeit when He, the Spirit of truth, is come, He will guide you into all truth: for He shall not speak of Himself; but whatsoever He shall hear, that shall He speak: and He will shew you things to come.

HEALING: We all need healing soon or later. Due to situation we get hurt our heart need healing our mind need healing as we get older many time our bodies need healing. God has made healing available for us. Psalms 147:3 He healeth the broken in heart, and bindeth up their wounds. James 5:13-16 Is any among you afflicted? Let him pray. Is any merry? Let him sing psalms. Is any sick among you? Let him call for the elders of the church; and let them pray over him, anointing him with oil in the name of the Lord. And the prayer of faith shall save the sick, and the Lord shall raise him up; and if he has committed sins, they shall be forgiven him. Confess your faults one to another, and pray one for another, that ye may be healed. The effectual fervent prayer of a righteous man availeth much.

PLEASING GOD: Since God has saved us from our sin it is our desire to please Him In every way. Hebrews 11:5-6 By Faith Enoch was translated that he should not see death; and was not found, because God had translated him; for before his translation he had this testimony, that he pleased God. But without faith it is impossible to please him: for him that cometh to God must believe that he is, and that he is a rewarder of them that diligently seek him.

Victory: We all want to be successful in living for the Lord and in everyday living. I John 5:4 Whatsoever is born of God overcometh the world; and this is the victory that overcometh the world, even our faith.

Understanding: Many things we don't understand. We accept them through faith. Through faith we understand that the worlds were frame by the word of God, so that things which are seen were not made of things which do appear.

WISDOM: We all need wisdom. Wisdom tells us how to apply knowledge. James 1:5-8 If any of you lack wisdom, let him ask of God, that giveth to all men liberally, and upbraideth not; and it shall be given him. But let him ask in faith, nothing wavering. For he that wavereth is like a wave of the seas driven with the wind and tossed. For let not that man think that he shall receive any thing of the Lord. A double minded man is unstable in all his ways . . .

In order for faith to work it must have love. Galatians 5:6 Faith work by love. Faith needs work to make it work. James 2:14-26 What doth it profit, my brethren, though a man say he hath faith, and have not works? Can faith save him? If a brother or sister be naked, and destitute of daily food. And one of you say unto them, Depart in peace, be ye warmed and filled; not withstanding ye give them not those things which are needful to the body; what doth it profit? Even so faith, if it hath not works, is dead, being alone. Yea, a man may say, Thou hast faith, and I have works:

show me thy faith without thy work, and I will show thee my faith by my works. Thou believest that there is one God; thou doest well: the devils also believe, and tremble. But wilt thou know, O vain man, that faith without works is dead? Was not Abraham our father justified by works, when he had offered Isaac his son upon the altar? Seeest thou how faith wrought with his works, and by works was faith made perfect? And the scripture was fulfilled which saith, Abraham believed God, and it was imputed unto him for righteousness; and he was called the friend of God, Ye see then how that by works a man is justified, and not by faith only. Likewise also was not Rahab the harlot justified by works, when she had received the messengers, and had sent them out another way? For as the body without the spirit is dead, so faith without works is dead also.

YES, I CAN REPENT—Repent is to feel sorry for what one has or has not done. We need to feel sorry enough that we will change our mind, will, and direction. Repent is a way of agreeing with the Lord and with the word of God. We ask the Lord to forgive us of our sin. I John 1:8-9 If we say that we have not sin, we deceive ourselves, and the truth is not in us. If we confess our sins, he is faithful and just to forgive us our sins, and to cleanse us from all unrighteousness. Romans 3:23 For all have sinned, and come short of the glory of God. Isaiah 1:18 Come now and let us reason together, saith the Lord; though your sins be as scarlet, they shall be as white as snow; though they be red like crimson, they shall be as wool. God want to reason with us. We need to confess and forsake our sin. Jesus know that we are not able to clean ourselves so He paid a price for our sins and we just need to come and confess to Him and be will to give up that sin to the Lord. Psalms 32:5 I acknowledged my sin unto thee, and mine iniquity have I not hid. I said, I will confess my transgressions unto the

Lord; and thou forgavest the iniquity of my sin. Proverbs 28:13 He that covered his sins shall not prosper; but whoso confessed and forsakes them shall have mercy.

We must repent in order to set it right with the Lord. John the Baptism preached repent Luke 3:3 And he came into all the country about Jordan, preaching the baptism of repentance for the remission of sins; Luke 13:1-3 There were present at that season some that told him of the Galileans, whose blood Pilate had mingled with their sacrifices. And Jesus answering said unto them, suppose that these Galileans were sinners above all the Galileans, because they suffered such things? I tell you, nay; except ye repent, ye shall all likewise perish. It doesn't matter what we have done God is willing to forgive our sin, He take our sins and put them in the sea of forgiven and He will remember our sin no more. He is full of grace and mercy.

Mark 1:14-15 Now after that John was put in prison, Jesus came into Galilee, preaching the gospel of the Kingdom of God, And saying, The time is fulfilled, and the Kingdom of God is at hand; repent ye and believe the gospel. Mark 2:16-17 And when the scribes and Pharisees saw Him (Jesus) eat with publicans and sinners, they said unto His disciples, How is it that He eateth and drinketh with publicans and sinners? When Jesus heard it, He saith unto them, they that are whole have no need of the physician, but they that are sick: I came not to call the righteous, but sinners to repentance.

Acts 17:30 And the times of this ignorance God winked at; but now commanded all men everywhere to repent. Repent is a command, we must repent to get it right with the Lord. 2 Peter 3:8-9 But beloved, be not ignorant of this one thing, that one day is with the Lord as a thousand years, and a thousand years as one day. The Lord is not slack concerning His promise, as some men count slackness; but is long suffering to us-ward, not willing that any should perish, but that all should come to repentance. It is not God willing for any of us to perish but that all should come to repent. Jesus died that we may have eternal life.

Luke 24:46-47 And said unto them, Thus it is written, and thus it behoved Christ to suffer, and to rise from the dead the third day; and that repentance and remission of sins should be preached in his name (Jesus) among all nations, beginning at Jerusalem. Acts 2:37-38 Now when they heard this, they were pricked in their heart, and said unto Peter and to the rest of the apostles, Men and brethren, what shall we do? Peter had preached the gospel and the people realized that the one that they had crucified is both Lord and Christ. And they ask the question what we must do. Then peter said unto them, Repent, and be baptized every one of you in the name of Jesus Christ for the remission of sins, and ye shall receive the gift of the Holy Ghost.

When we believe we must repent. 2 Corinthians 7:9-11 Now I rejoice, not that ye were made sorry, but that ye sorrowed to repentance; for ye were made sorry after a godly manner, that ye might receive damage by us in nothing. For godly sorrow worked repentance to salvation not to be repented of: but the sorrow of the world worked death. For behold this selfsame thing, that ye sorrowed after a godly sort, what carefulness it wrought in you, yea, what clearing of yourselves, yea, what indignation, yea, what fear, yea, what vehement desire, yea, what zeal, yea, what revenge! In all things ye have approved yourselves to be clear in this matter. Godly repent will worked fruit of righteousness in our life.

Carefulness-you will watch yourselves so that you will not sin. Psalms 141:3 Set a watch, O Lord, before my mouth, keep the door of my lips.

Clearing—free of guilt or condemnation. Romans 8:1 There is therefore now no condemnation to them which are in Christ Jesus, who walk not after the flesh, but after the Spirit.

Indignation-we learn to hatred sin. Psalm 119:104 Through thy precepts I get understand: therefore I hate every false way.

Fear—of God and sin result. Proverbs 8:13 The fear of the Lord is to hate evil: pride, and arrogancy, and the evil way, and the forward mouth, do I hate.

Vehement Desire. To be righteous and to obey God's Word. Matthew 5:6 Blessed are they that hunger and thirst after righteousness; for they shall be filled.

Zeal—In working for God and His cause. Ephesians 6:5-7 Servants, be obedient to them that are your masters according to the flesh, with fear and trembling, in singleness of your heart, as unto Christ; Not with eyeservice, as menpleasers; but as the servants of Christ, doing the will of God from the heart. With good will doing service, as to the Lord, and not to men.

Revenge-acknowledging justice and the punishment of sin. Matthew 18:26 The servant therefore fell down, and worshipped Him, saying Lord, have patience with me, and I will pay thee all. Then the lord of that servant was moved with compassion, and loosed him, and forgave him the debt. When godly repentance takes place there will be a desire to correct any wrong.

There are two type of repentance mention in the Bible.

Metamellomai—is a Greek word meaning to regret, to care afterward, and to be sorry for.

Metanaeo-a Greek word meaning to think differently, to change one's mind, purpose, or opinion.

2 Corinthians 7:8-10 For though I made you sorry with a letter; I do not repent(He has not change his mind): though I did repent(I did feel sorry): For I perceive that the same epistle hath made you sorry, though it were but for a season. Now I rejoice, not that ye were made sorry, but that ye sorrowed to repentance; for ye were made sorry after a godly manner, that ye might receive damage by us in nothing. For the godly sorrow worked repentance to salvation (change of mind) not to be repented of: (we are not to feel sorry after we have repented godly) but the sorrow of the world worked death.

Just feeling sorry for something we have done is not godly repenting. Godly repent agree with God that what we have done is against His commandment and there is a change of mind, direction, and purpose. People are sorry because they got caught and if they get a chance to do it again and think they can get by with it they will do it again. Godly repent there is a change of mind and direction and if you get a chance to do it again and believe that you can get by with it you won't do because there is a change of mind. God wants you and me to repent Godly. In Godly repent there is a confessing and a forsaking of sin and we find the grace of God and forgiveness from the Lord.

YES, I CAN FORGIVE—Yes, I can forgive because the Lord has forgiven me. Psalms 103:3 Who forgiveth all thine iniquities; who healeth all thy diseases. Ezekiel 18:22 But there is forgiveness with thee, that thou mayest be fear. Matthews 6:14 For if ye forgive men their trespasses, your Heavenly Father will also forgive you. But if ye forgive not men their trespasses, neither will your Father forgive your trespasses. If you and I refuse to forgive other then we hinder our forgiveness from the Lord.

Acts 5:30-31 The God of our Fathers raised up Jesus, whom ye slew and hanged on a tree. Him hath God exalted with his right hand to be a Prince and a Saviour, for to give repentance to Israel, and forgiveness of sins. It is God will, that we repent and find forgiveness of sin. 2 Peter 3:8-9 But, beloved, be not ignorant of this one thing, that one day is with the Lord as a thousand years, and a thousand years as one day. The Lord is not slack concerning His promise, as some men count slackness; but is longsuffering to us-ward, not willing that any should perish, but that all should come to repentance. Ephesians 1:7 In whom we have redemption through His blood, the forgiveness of sins, according to the riches of His grace;

I John 7-10 But if we walk in the light, as He is in the light, we have fellowship one with another, and the blood of Jesus Christ His Son cleanseth us from all sin. If we say that we have no sin, we deceive ourselves, and the truth is not in us. If we confess our sins, He is faithful and just to forgive us our sins, and to cleanse us from all unrighteousness. If we say that we have not sinned, we make Him a liar, and His word is not in us. When we confess our sin God not only forgives us but cleanness us from all sin. Because Jesus has forgiven us it encourages us to forgive other. When we remember what Jesus went through for us, and how He forgave us. It helps us to forgive us. Hebrew 12:2-4 Looking unto Jesus the author and finisher of our faith; who for the joy that was set before Him endured the cross, despising the shame, and is set down at the right hand of the throne of God. For consider Him that endured such contradiction of sinners against Himself, lest ye be wearied and faint in your mind. Ye have not yet resisted unto blood, striving against sin. Keep your eyes upon Jesus, and it becomes easier to forgive.

When we forgive relationship is healed, emotional heal take place for you and the other person. I John 1:7 But if we walk in the light, as He is in the light, we have fellowship one with another, and the blood of Jesus Christ His Son cleanseth us from all sin. Husband and wives and other family relationship can be restored when forgiveness take place.

Matthew 6:14-15 For if ye forgive men their trespasses, your Heavenly Father will also forgive you. But if ye forgive not men their trespasses, neither will your Father forgive your trespasses. When we forgive God is able to forgive us.

Our sin will not be retained when we choose to forgive. Matthew 18:23-35 Therefore is the Kingdom of heaven likened unto a certain king, which would take account of his servant. And when he had begun to reckon, one was brought unto him, which owed him ten thousand talents. But forasmuch as he had not to pay, his lord commanded him to be sold, and his wife, and his children, and all that he had, and payment to be made. The servant therefore fell down, and worshipped him, saying, Lord, have patience with me, and I will pay thee all. Then the lord of that servant was moved with compassion, and loosed him, and forgave him the debt. But the same servant went out, and found one of his fellowservants, which owed him an hundred pence: and took him by the throat, saying, pay me that thou owest. And his fellowservant fell down at his feet, and besought him, saying, have patience with me, and I will pay thee all. And he would not: but went and cast him into prison, till he should pay the debt. So when his fellowservants saw what was done, they were very sorry, and came and told unto their lord all that was done. Then his lord, after that he had called him, said unto him, O thou wicked servant, I forgave thee all that debt, because thou desiredst me; Shouldest not thou also have compassion on thy fellowservant, even as I had pity on thee? And his lord was wroth, and delivered him to the tormentors, till he should pay all that was due unto him. So likewise shall my Heavenly Father do also unto you, if ye from your hearts forgive not everyone his brother their trespasses. When we forgive our sins are not retained and God doesn't call us the wicked servant.

When we don't forgive our sin are not forgiven, relationships are broken, and healings are hinder. And unforgiveness can hinder your prayer life.

YES, I CAN READ MY BIBLE EVERYDAY-The Word **of** God is God. I John 1:1 In the beginning was the Word, and the Word was with God, and the Word was God. When we read the word of God, we are allowing God to talk to us. God is saying I will heal you; I forgive all your iniquities. I healed all your diseases. God is right there to minister to your need. Saying you can do all things through Christ, who strength you. God is right there to minister to any need you have because the Word of God is God;

Psalm 19:7-11 The law of the Lord is perfect, converting the soul: the testimony of the Lord is sure, making wise the simple, The statutes of the Lord are right, rejoicing the heart; the commandment of the Lord is pure, enlightening the eyes, the fear of the Lord is clean, enduring forever:

the judgments of the Lord are true and righteous altogether. More to be desired are they than gold, yea, than much fine gold; sweeter also than honey and the honeycomb. Moreover by them is thy servant warned: and in keeping of them there is great reward. The word of God will change your life. You can become a new creature, the word of God will make you wise and give you enlighten, and make your heart rejoices. Everything that we need is in the Word of God.

I Peter 2:1-3 Wherefore laying aside all malice, and guile, and hypocrisies, and envies, and all evil speakings. As newborn babes, desire the sincere milk of the Word that ye may grow thereby: If so be ye have tasted that the Lord is gracious. As in the natural baby maybe born a normal healthy baby but if the baby is not is not feed the baby become weak and if something is not done the baby will eventually die. For a baby must be feed. This is true regarding us as baby in Christ if we don't eat the milk of the word we will become weak and if we are not feed we will backslide. The Bible say as newborn babies desire the sincere milk of the word so we can grow thereby. My doctor told me to feed my baby every four hours. How often do we read the word of God to stay spiritually health? In order for us to grow in the Lord, we need the word of God every day. We don't need to wait until we get to the House of the Lord. If we read three chapters a day and five chapters on Sunday; you can read the entire Bible in one year and it only take fifteen to twenty minute a day. You can read the entire New testament by spend twenty minute a day in the New Testament. It is best to start in the New Testament first to get understanding.

Job 23:10-12 But He knoweth the way that I take; when He hath tried me, I shall come forth as gold. My foot hath held His steps, His way have I kept, and not declined. Neither have I gone back from the commandment of his lips, I have esteemed the words of His mouth more than my necessary food. When Job went through his trial and, the thing that kept Job was the word of God. It is going to take the word of God to keep you and me for without the word of God we will surely die.

We need natural food to keep the body healthy. Job consist the Word of God more important than natural food. We eat three times a day and let not forget about the between snack that we feel we must have. How many times a day do we read the word of God? Job said I have esteem thou word more necessary than my daily food. Can we say that the word of God is more important than our daily food? Matthew 4:1-11 Then was Jesus led up of the Spirit into the wilderness to be tempted of the devil. And when He had fasted forty days and forty nights, He was afterward a hungred. And when the tempter came to Him, he said, if thou be the Son of God, command that these stones be made bread. But He answered and said, it is written, Man shall not live by bread alone, but by every word that proceedeth out of the mouth of God. Then the devil taketh Him up into the Holy city, and setteth Him on a pinnacle of the temple, And saith unto Him, If thou be the Son of God, cast thyself down: for it is written, He shall give His angels charge concerning thee: and in their hands they shall bear thee up, lest at any time thou dash thy foot against a stone. Jesus said unto Him, It is written again, Thou shalt not tempt the Lord thy God. Again, the devil taketh him up into an exceeding high mountain, and sheweth him all the kingdoms of the world, and the glory of them. And saith unto Him, All these things will I give thee, if thou will fall down and worship me. Then saith Jesus unto him, Get the hence, satan; for it is written, Thou shalt worship the Lord thy God, and Him only shalt thou serve. Then the devil leaveth Him, and behold, angels came and ministered unto Him. Jesus used the Word of God to overcome the devil we can also use the word of God to overcome the devil.

God word has been tested, trialed, and prove. Psalm 119:89 For ever, O Lord, thy word is settled in heaven. God word will never fail us. Matthew 24:35 Heaven and earth shall pass away, but my words shall not pass away. 2Peter 1:19-21 We have also a more sure word of prophecy; whereunto ye do well that ye take heed, as unto a light that shineth in a dark place, until the day dawn, and the day star arise in your hearts: Knowing this first, that no prophecy of the scripture is of any private interpretation. For the prophecy came not in old time by the will of man: but holy men of God spake as they were moved by the Holy Ghost. I Peter 1:22-25 Seeing ye have purified your souls in obeying the truth through the Spirit unto unfeigned love of the brethren, see that ye love one another with a pure heart fervently: Being born again, not of corruptible seed, but of incorruptible, by the word of God, which liveth and abideth forever. For all flesh is as grass, and all the glory of man as the flower of grass. The grass withereth, and the flower thereof falleth away; but the word of the Lord endureth forever. And this is the word which by the gospel is preached unto you. Matthew 5:18 For verily I say unto you, till heaven and earth pass, one jot or one tittle shall in no wise pass from the law, till all be fulfilled.

Many times we put interest in dream. Jeremiah 23:28-32 The prophet that hath a dream, let him tell a dream; and he that hath my word, let him speak my word faithfully. What is the chaff to the wheat? Saith the Lord. Is not my word like as a fire? Saith the Lord; and like a hammer that breaketh the rock in pieces? Therefore, behold, I am against the prophets, saith the Lord, that steal my words everyone from his neighbour. Behold, I am against the prophets, saith the Lord, that use their tongues, and say,

He saith. Behold, I am against them that prophesy false dreams, saith the Lord, and do tell them, and cause my people to err by their lies, and by their lightness, yet I sent them not, nor commanded them: therefore they shall not profit this people at all. Saith the Lord. A dream is a dream but the Word of the Lord is right and trialed.

2 Timothy 3:15-17 And that from a child thou hast known the Holy Scriptures, which are able to make thee wise unto salvation through faith which is in Christ Jesus. All scripture is given by inspiration of God, and is profitable for doctrine, for reproof, for correction, for instruction in righteousness; that the man of God may be perfect, throughly furnished unto all good works. The Word of God is profitable for doctrine, for reproof, for correction, and for instruction in righteousness.

Doctrine—teaches what is right. It is to be used to teach, instruct and direct us in settled Bible truths. Isaiah 28:9-13 Whom shall He teach knowledge? And whom shall He make to understand doctrine? Them that are weaned from the milk, and drawn from the breasts. For precept must be upon precept, precept upon precept; line upon line, line upon line; here a little, and there a little; for with stammering lip; and another tongue, will He speak to this people. To whom He said, this is the rest wherewith ye may cause the weary to rest; and this the refreshing; yet they would not hear. But the word of the Lord was unto them precept upon precept, precept upon precept, line upon line, line upon line, here a little, and there a little; that they might go, and fall backward, and be broken, and snared, and taken. ITimothy 4:13-16 Till I come, give attendance to reading, to exhortation, to doctrine. Neglect not the gift that is in thee, which was given thee by prophecy, with the laying on of the hands of the presbytery. Meditate upon these things; give thyself wholly to them;

that thy profiting may appear to all. Take heed unto thyself, and unto the doctrine, continue in them: for in doing this thou shalt both save thyself, and them that hear thee.

Reproof—teaches us what is wrong. It shows us our fault. What is wrong in our life, in the church and what is wrong in our home. The Word of God will rebuke us when sin is in our life. Proverbs 1:23-30 Turn you at my reproof: behold, I will pour out my Spirit unto you. I will make known my words unto you. Because I have called, and ye refused: I have stretch out my hand, and no one man regarded. But ye have set at nought all my counsel, and would none of my reproof: I also will laugh at your calamity; I will mock when fear cometh; when your fear cometh as desolation and your destruction cometh as a whirlwind; when distress and anguish cometh upon you. Then shall they call upon me, but I will not answer; they shall seek me early, but they shall not find me. For that they hated knowledge, and did not choose the fear of the Lord; they would none of my counsel; they despised all my reproof.

Correction—Word of God correct thing that is wrong in the home, church and things that is wrong in our life. It will correct false theories. Proverb 3:11-12 My son, despise not the chastening of the Lord, neither be weary of His correction. For whom the Lord loveth he correcteth, even as a father the son in whom he delighteth. Job 5:17 Behold, happy is the man whom God correcteth: therefore despise not thou the chastening of the Almighty. Jeremiah 2:30 In vain have I smitten your children they received no correction; your own sword hath devoured your prophets, like a destroying lion. Hebrew 12:6-11 For whom the Lord loveth he chasteneth, and scourgeth every son whom he receiveth. If ye endure chastening. God dealeth with you as with sons; for what son is he whom the father chasteneth not? But if ye be without chastisement, whereof all are partakers, then are ye bastards, and not sons. Furthermore we have had fathers of our flesh which corrected us, and we gave them reverence: shall we not much rather is in subjection unto the Father of Spirits, and live? For they verily for a few days chastened us after their own pleasure; but he for our profit, that we might be partakers of his holiness. Now no chastening for the present seemeth to be joyous, but grievous: nevertheless afterward it yieldeth the peaceable fruit of righteousness unto them which are exercised thereby.

Instruction in Righteousness—The word of God teaches us how to stay right. Word of God is just like a school, you never stop learn; the more you learn the more you realize that you need to know. Matthew 13:52 Then said he unto them, Therefore every scribe which is instructed unto the kingdom of is like unto a man that is an householder, which bringeth forth out of his treasure things new and old. 2 Timothy 2:25-26 In meekness instructing those that oppose themselves; if God peradventure will give them repentance to the acknowledging of the truth; And that they may recover themselves out of the snare of the devil, who are taken captive by him at his will. Acts 18:24-28 And a certain Jew named Apollos, born at Alexandria, and eloquent man, and mighty in the scriptures, came to Ephesus. This man was instructed in the way of the Lord; and being fervent in the spirit, he spake and taught diligently the things of the Lord, knowing only the baptism of John. And he began to speak boldly in the synagogue: whom when Aquila and Priscilla had heard, they took him unto them, and expounded unto him the way of God more perfectly. And when he was disposed to pass into Achia, the brethren wrote, exhorting the disciples to receive him; who, when he was come, helped them much which had believed through grace; for he mightily convinced the Jews, and that publickly, shewing by the scriptures that Jesus was Christ. The Word of God is our school that we are always learning.

The word of God is our light in a dark place. Psalm 19:8 The statues of the Lord are right, rejoicing the heart; the commandment of the Lord is pure, enlightening the eyes In the darkness the word of the Lord will give us light and it will bring joy to our heart. In the greatness darkness, there is light the Word of God. The Word of God gives us light and direction. Psalm 119:105 Thy word is a lamp unto my feet, and a light into my path.

The word of God move confusion. Psalm 119:130 The entrance of thy words giveth light; it giveth understanding unto the simple.

The saint of God fall in love with the Word of God, Psalm 119:47 And I will delight myself in thy commandments, which I have loved Psalm 119:72 The law of thy mouth is better unto me than thousands of gold and silver. Psalm 119:97 O how loves I thy law! It is my meditation all the day. Psalm 119:140 Thy word is very pure: therefore thy servant loveth it. Psalm 119:82 Mine eyes fall for they word saying when wilt thou comfort me? Jeremiah 15:16 Thy words were found, and I did eat them; and thy word was unto me the joy and rejoicing of mine heart; for I am called by thy name, O Lord God of hosts. Psalm 119:161-164 Princes have persecuted me without a cause: but my heart standeth in awe of thy word. I rejoice at thy word, as one that findeth great spoil. I hate and abhor lying; but thy law do I love. Seven times a day do I praise thee because of thy righteous judgments? Psalm 119:126-128 It is time for thee, Lord, to work: for they have made void thy law. Therefore I love thy commandments above gold; yea, above fine gold. Therefore I esteem all thy precepts concerning all things to be right; and I hate every false way. The saint of God love the word of God for the word of God is our hope.

The Word of God will be in our heart. Deuteronomy 6:6 And these words, which I command thee this day, shall be in thine heart; Deuteronomy 11:18 Therefore shall ye lay up these my words in your heart and in your soul and bind them for a sign upon your hand, that they may be as frontlets between your eyes. Psalm 119:11 Thy Word have I hid in mine heart, that I might not sin against thee. Romans 10:8 But what saith it? The word is nigh thee, even in thy mouth, and in thy heart; that is, the word of faith, which we preach. Colossians 3:16 Let the Word of Christ dwell in you richly in all wisdom, teaching and admonishing one another in psalms and hymns and spiritual songs, singing with grace in your hearts to the Lord. Psalm 37:30 The mouth of the righteous speaketh wisdom, and his tongue talketh of judgment. The law of his God is in his heart; none of his steps shall slide. Psalm 40:8 I delight to do thy will, O my God: yea, thy law is within my heart. Hebrews 10:16-17 This is the covenant that I will make with them after those days, saith the Lord, I will put my laws into their hearts, and in their minds will I write them; And their sins and iniquities will I remember no more.

Commit to memory inspirational and salvation-related scripture. When I am going through I just memorized the word of God. Psalm 37, Psalm 91 and memorized scripture on financial Sometime I memorize scripture on prayer, and peace. And when confusion or dark day comes, you will have the treasure of God word inside of you. God always come through for me.

The Word of God will purify your life. Psalm 119:9 Wherewithal shall a young man cleanse his way? By taking heed thereto according to thy word.

John 15:3 Now ye are clean through the word which I have spoken unto you. John 17:18 sanctify them through truth; thy word is truth. Ephesians 5:26 That He might sanctify and cleanse it with the washing of water by the word.

We are sanctified by the Holy Spirit and by the Word of God. John 3:1-8 There was a man of the Pharisees, named Nicodemus, a ruler of the Jews: The same came to Jesus by night, and said unto Him, Rabbi, we know that thou art a teacher come from God; for no man can do these miracles that thou doest, except God be with him. Jesus answered and said unto him, Verily, verily, I say unto thee, Except a man be born again, he cannot see the kingdom of God. Nicodemus saith unto Him, How can a man be born when he is old? Can he enter the second time into his mother's womb, and be born? Jesus answered, Verily, Verily I say unto thee, except a man is born of water and of the Spirit, he cannot enter into the Kingdom of God. That which is born of the flesh is flesh; and that which is born of the Spirit is spirit. Marvel not that I said unto thee, ye must be born again. The wind bloweth where it listeth, and thou hearest the sound thereof, but canst not tell whence it cometh, and whither it goeth: so is everyone that is born of the Spirit.

The Word of God and the Holy Spirit word together sanctified us. I Corinthians 12:13 For by one Spirit are we all baptized into one body, whether we be Jews or Gentiles, whether we be bond or free; and have been all made to drink into one Spirit. Word of God cleans and purifies us. Matthew 22:29 Jesus answered and said unto them, ye do err, not knowing the scriptures, nor the power of God. To live a holy sanctified life it takes both the Spirit of God and the Word of God.

Why should we read and study the Word of God. We read the word to allow God to put his word in our heart. If we don't read and study the word of God, the word of God will not be in our heart. For faith without work is dead.

2 Timothy 2:15-16 Study to shew thyself approved unto God, a workman that needeth not to be ashamed, rightly dividing the word of truth. But shun profane and vain babbllings: for they will increase unto more ungodliness. We need to study the word of God simple because God says for us to study the Word of God, that we will not be ashamed, to be approving to God and to learn to right divide the word of truth.

I Peter 3:15-16 But sanctify the Lord God in your hearts: and be ready always to give an answer to every man that asketh you a reason of the hope that is in you with meekness and fear. Having a good conscience; that, whereas they speak evil of you, as of evildoers, they may be an ashamed that falsely accuse your good conversation in Christ. The Word of God equips us with answer, so when we speak we will be able to make those that false accuse us feel asham.

Psalm 71:21Thou shalt increase my greatness, and comfort me on every side. One thing I love about the Word of God, the word of God always comfort me. Psalm 23:4 Yea, though I walk through the valley of the shadow of death, I will fear no evil: for thou art with me; thy rod and thy staff they comfort me.

Psalm 119:11 Thy word has I hid in mine heart, that I might not sin against thee. The word of God cleans you and me. Psalm 119:9 Wherewithal shall a young man cleanse his way? By taking heed thereto according to thy word.

Ephesians 6:17 And take the helmet of Salvation, and the sword of the Spirit, which is the word of God. The Holy Ghost is the power of God. The word of God is the sword of the Spirit. The word of God is what we fight with. The word tells us who we are a new creature in Christ Jesus. We need to have the Word of God in our heart not just in our hands, to call to remember the word of God when we go though trial.

Isaiah 28:9-13 Whom shall he teach knowledge? And whom shall he make to understand doctrine? Them that are weaned from the milk, and drawn from the breasts. For precept must be upon precept, precept upon precept; line upon line, line upon line; here a little; and there a little: For with stammering lips and another tongue will he speak to this people. To whom he said, This is the rest wherewith ye may cause the weary to rest; and this the refreshing: yet they would not hear. But the Word of the Lord was unto them precept upon precept, precept upon precept; line upon line, line upon line; here a little and there a little; that they might go, and fall backward, and be broken, and snared and taken. We need to read and study the Word of God because of the structure of the Word of God. The Word of God can be used to explain itself. Compare scripture with scripture. A line is rule, and connecting form, precept is the commandment of God. Here a little, there a little mean you will not find the entire subject matter in one place we need to move around that is why we need a good study Bible. I recommend the Thompson Chain Reference Bible.

2 Timothy 2:2 And the things that thou hast heard of me among many witnesses, the same commit thou to faithful men, who shall be able to teach others also. Study the word of God because it equips you and me to teach other. Hebrews 5:12-14 For when for the time ye ought to be teachers,

ye heave need that one teach you again which is the first principles of the oracles of God; and are become such as have need of milk, and not of strong meat. For everyone that useth milk is unskillful in the word of righteousness: for he is a babe. But strong meat belongeth to them that are of full age, even those who by reason of use have their senses exercised to discern both good and evil.

YES, I CAN PRAY EVERYDAY. Prayer is simply communication with God. In order to be an overcomer we must pray. Pray every day and all through the day. You don't need to be on your knees in order to pray. You can stand, lie, sit or walk. Just pray. I Thessalonians 5:17 Pray without ceasing. Never stop praying. God invites us to pray, pray with you family and your friend. Jeremiah 33: Call unto me, and I will answer thee, and show thee great and mighty things, which thou knowest not.

Matthew 6:5-13 And when thou prayest, thou shalt not be as the hypocrites are: for they love to pray standing in the synagogues and in the corners of the streets, that they may be seen of men. Verily I say unto you, they have their reward. But thou, when thou prayest, enter into thy closet, and when thou hast shut thy door, pray to thou Father which is in secret: and thy Father which seeth in secret shall reward thee openly. But when ye pray, use not vain repetitions, as the heathen do; for they think that they shall be heard for their much speaking. Be not ye therefore like unto them: for your Father knoweth what things ye have need of, before ye ask Him. After this manner therefore pray ye: Our Father which art in heaven, Hallowed be thy name. Thy kingdom come. Thy will be done in earth, as it is in heaven. Give us this day our daily bread. And forgive us our debts, as we forgive our debtors. And lead us not into temptation, but deliver us from evil; For thine is the Kingdom and the power, and the glory, forever Amen.

Develop a consistent pray life every day and all through the day. Luke 11:1-13 And it came to pass, that, as He was praying in a certain place, when he ceased, one of His disciples said unto him, Lord, teach us to pray, as John also taught His disciples. And He said unto them, when ye pray, say, Our Father which art in heaven, Hallowed be thy name. Thy kingdom come. Thy will be done, as in heaven, so in earth. Give us day by day our daily bread. And forgive us our sins; for we also forgive every one that is indebted to us. And lead us not into temptation; but deliver us from evil. And He said unto them, which of you shall have a friend, and shall go unto him at midnight, and say unto him, Friend, lend me three loaves; For a friend of mine in his journey is come to me, and I have nothing to set before Him? And he from within shall answer and say, Trouble me not: the door is now shut, and my children are with me in bed; I cannot rise and give thee. I say unto you, though he will not rise and give him, because he is his friend, yet because of his importunity he will rise and give him as many as he needeth. And I say unto you, Ask and it shall be given you; seek, and ye shall find; knock, and it shall be opened unto you. For every one that asketh receiveth; and he that seeketh findeth; and to him that knocketh it shall be opened. If a son shall ask bread of any of you that is a father, will he give him a stone? Or if he asks a fish, will he for a fish give him a serpent? Or if he shall ask an egg, will he offer him a scorpion? If ye then, being evil, know how to give good gifts unto your children; how much more shall your heavenly Father give the Holy Spirit to them that ask Him? Never! Never! Give up in prayer for the Lord will answer you.

James 5: 13-18 Is any among you afflicted? Let him pray. Is any merry? Let him sing psalms. Is any sick among you? Let him call for the elders of the church; and let them pray over him, anointing him with oil in the name of the Lord; and the prayer of faith shall save the sick and the Lord shall raise him up; and if he has committed sins, they shall be forgiven him. Confess your faults one to another, and pray one for another, that ye may be healed. The effectual fervent prayer of a righteous man availeth much. Elias was a man subject to like passions as we are, and he prayed earnestly that it might not rain: and it rained not on the earth by the space of three years and six months. And he prayed again, and the heaven gave rain, and the earth brought forth her fruit. Call for the elder, if you are sick that is an act of faith.

If we ever realize the unlimited power of prayers, we will see mountain move, the dead raise, and sick bodies heal. Mark 11:22-24 And Jesus answering saith unto them have faith in God. For verily I say unto you, That whosoever shall say unto this mountain, Be thou removed, and be thou cast into the sea; and shall not doubt in his heart, but shall believe that those things which he saith shall come to pass; he shall have whatsoever he saith Therefore I say unto you, What things soever ye desire, when ye pray, believe that ye receive them and ye shall have them.

James 5:17 Elias was a man subject to like passions as we are, and he prayed earnestly that it might not rain: and it rained not on the earth by the space of three year and six months. I could not find anywhere in the Bible where Elias real prayed that it not rain on the earth But Elias spoken the word **and** it rain not on the earth for a space of three year and six month. I King 17:1 And Elijah the Tishbite, who was of the inhabitants of Gilead, said unto Ahab, As the Lord God of Israel liveth, before whom

I stand; there shall not be dew nor rain these years, but according to my word. Was Elias prayer just simply speaking the word? Is this what God call earnestly prayer, just speaking the word?

Alone with prayer faith must be enjoin. Faith is the key to the power of prayer. John 10:10 The thief cometh not, but to steal, and to kill, and to destroy: I am come that they might have life, and that they might have it more abundantly. We must guard our faith less we allow the devil to steal our faith. The Bible say Jesus is the author and finisher of our faith. Hebrews 11:6 But without faith it is impossible to please Him: for he that cometh to God, must believe that He is, and that He is a rewarder of them that diligently seek him.

James 5:17-18 Elias was a man subject to like passions as we are, and he prayed earnestly that it might not rain: and it rained not on the earth by the space of three years and six months. And he prayed again, and the earth brought forth her fruit. We may think Elias was man without fault or weakness, but the Bible say he was subject to passion as we are. Yet he just spoke the word and it didn't rain for three years and and a half. If we assume that Elias was without fault and passions that can hinder our faith but if we can see that Elias was weak and with passions we can believe that God will answer our Prayers.

We all need to pray I Timothy 2:8 I will therefore that men pray everywhere, lifting up holy hands, without wrath and doubting. We are to pray everywhere on the bus, in the classroom everywhere and anywhere, we are to pray without ceasing.

James 5:16 The effectual fervent prayer of a righteous man availeth much. When our heart is right with God, it causes the Lord to hear our prayers. If there is unforgiveness in our heart we need to get rid of it.

We are to always pray. Luke 18:1 And he spake a parable unto them to this end, that men ought always to pray, and not to faint.

Jude 20 But ye, beloved, building up yourselves on your most holy faith, praying in the Holy Ghost. When we pray in the spirit we build ourselves up. I love to pray in the Spirit the Bible says we real don't know how to pray as we ought. Romans 8:26-28 Likewise the spirit also help our infirmities: for we know not what we should pray for as we ought; But the spirit itself maketh intercession for us with groaning which cannot be uttered. And He that searcheth the hearts knoweth what is the mind of the Spirit, because he maketh intercession for the saints according to the will of God. And we know that all things work together for good to them that love God, to them who are the called according to His purpose. When we pray in the Spirit we know our prayers are being heard because we are praying according to the will of God. I John 5:14-15 And this is the confidence that we have in Him, that, if we ask anything according to His will, He heareth us. And if we know that He hear us, whatsoever we ask, we know that we has the petitions that we desired of Him.

I Peter 5:7 Casting all your care upon Him; for He careth for you. When we pray we are talking to someone who really cares about us. We can tell Him anything we like and He won't share it with anyone else. Philippians 4:6 Be careful for nothing, but in everything by prayer and supplication with thanksgiving let your requests be made known unto God. And the peace of God, which passeth all understanding, shall keep your hearts and minds through Christ Jesus. We need to cast all our care upon the Lord, because he care for us and then and only then can we have the peace of God in our life

Matthew 18:18-20 Verily I say unto you, Whatsoever ye shall bind on earth shall be bound in heaven and whatsoever ye shall loose on earth shall be loosed in heaven. Again I say unto you, That if two of you shall agree on earth as touching anything that they shall ask, it shall be done for them of my Father which is in heaven. For where two or three are gathered together in my name, there am I in the midst of them. There are times when we need to gather together and pray and rebuke the devil in Jesus name. Ecclesiastes 4:9-12 Two are better than one; because they have a good reward for their labour. For if they fall, the one will lift up his fellow but woe to him that is alone when he falleth, for he hath not another to help him up. Again, if two lie together, they have heat, but how can one be warm alone? And if one prevails against him, two shall withstand him; and a threefold cord is not quickly broken.

AS you and I have special prayer request also did Jesus. Matthew 9:38 Pray ye therefore the Lord of the harvest, that He will send forth labourers unto His harvest. Luke 21:36 Watch ye therefore, and pray always, that ye may be accounted worthy to escape all these thing that shall come to pass, and to stand before the Son of man,

There is difference type of prayers. There is the prayer of agreement where two or three are gather together in his name. I Timothy 2:1-2 I exhort therefore, that first of all, supplications, prayers, intercessions, and giving of thanks, be made for all men, for kings and for all that are in authority; that we may lead a quiet and peaceable life in all godliness and honest.

Hebrews 4:15-16 For we have not an high priest which cannot be touched with the feeling of our infirmities; but was in all points tempted like as we are, yet without sin. Let us therefore come boldly unto the throne of grace that we may obtain mercy, and find grace to help in time of need. We can come boldly to the throne of grace and fine mercy and help in a time of need.

We are to always put God first in our life. Matthew 6:33 But seek ye first the king of God, and His righteous ness; and all these things shall be added unto you. Colossians 3:1-5 If ye then be risen with Christ, seek those things which are above, where Christ setteth on the right hand of God. Set your affection on things above, not on thing on the earth. For ye are dead, and your life is hid with Christ in God. When Christ, who is our life, then shall ye also appear with him in glory. Mortify therefore your members which are upon the earth; fornication, uncleanness, inordinate affection, evil concupiscence. And covetousness, which is idolatry.

Never give up in your prayer especially if you know you are praying according to the will of God. Luke 18:1-8 And He spake a parable unto them to this end, that men ought to always to pray, and not to faint; Saying, There was in a city a judge, which feared not God, neither regarded man. And there was a widow in that city; and she came unto him saying. Avenge me of mine adversary. And he would not for a while: But afterward he said within himself, Though I fear not God, nor regard man; Yet Because this widow troubleth me, I will avenge her, lest by her continual coming she weary me. And the Lord said, Hear what the unjust judge saith. And shall not God avenge his own elect, which cry day and night unto Him, though he bears long with them? I tell you that he will avenge them speedily. Nevertheless when the Son of man cometh, shall he find faith on the earth?

Never think of yourself better than other in prayer for we are the righteousness of God by faith. Luke 18:9-14 And He spake this parable unto certain which trusted in themselves that they were righteous and despised others; Two men went up into the temple to pray; the one a Pharisee, and the other a publican. The Pharisee stood and prayed thus with himself, God I thank thee that I am not as other men are, extortioners, unjust, adulterers or even as this publican I fast twice in the week. I give tithes of all that I possess. And the publican, standing afar off, would not lift up so much as his eyes unto heaven, but smote upon his breast, saying. God be merciful to me a sinner. I tell you, this man went down to his house justified rather than the other; for every one that exalteth himself shall be abased; and he that humbleth himself shall be exalted.

Always keep a forgive spirit. Matthew 6:14-15 For if ye forgive men their trespasses, your heavenly Father will also forgive you: But if ye forgive not men their trespasses, neither will your Father forgive your trespasses. Matthew 6:12 And forgive us our debts as we forgive our debtors. Ephesians 4:31-32 Let all bitterness, and wrath, and anger, and clamour, and evil speaking, be put away from you, with all malice: And be ye kind one to another, tenderhearted, forgiving one another even as God for Christ 's sake hath forgiven you.

Our food is sanctified by prayer and the Word of God. I Timothy 4:4-6 For every creature of God is good, and nothing to be refused, if it be received with thanksgiving. For it is sanctified by the word of God and prayer.

Prayer can open prison door. Acts12:1-17 Now about that time Herod the king stretched forth his hands to vex certain of the church. And he killed James the brother of John with the sword. And because he saw it pleased the Jews, he proceeded further to take Peter also. (Then were the days of unleavened bread.) And when he had apprehended him, he put him in prison, and delivered him to four quaternions of soldier to keep him; intending after Easter to bring him forth to the people. Peter therefore was kept in prison: but prayer was made without ceasing of the church unto God for him. And when Herod would have brought him forth, the same night Peter was sleeping between two soldiers, bound with two chains: and the keepers before the door kept the prison. And behold, the angel of the Lord came upon him, and a light shinned in the prison: and he smote Peter on the side, and raised him up, saying, Arise up quickly. And his chain fell off from his hands. And the angel said unto him, Gird thyself, and bind on thy sandals. And so he did. And he saith unto him. Cast thy garment about thee, and follow me. And he went out, and followed him; and wist not that it was true which was done by the angel, but thought he saw a vision. When they were past the first and second ward, they came unto the iron gate that leadeth unto the city; which opened to them of his own accord: and they went out, and passed on through one street: and forthwith the angel departed from him. And when Peter was come to himself, he said; now I know of a surety, that the Lord hath sent his angel, and hath delivered me out of the hand of Herod, and from all the expectation of the people of the Jews. And when he had considered the thing, he came to the house of Mary the mother of John, whose surname was Mark: where many were gathered together praying. And as Peter knocked at the door of the gate, a damsel came to hearken, named Rhoda. And when she knew Peter's voice, she opened not the gate for gladness, but rain in, and told how Peter stood before the gate. And they said unto her, Thou art mad. But she constantly affirmed that it was even so. Then said they, it is his angel. But Peter continued knocking: and when they when they had opened the door, and saw him, they were astonished. But he, beckoning unto them with the hand to hold their peace, declared unto them how the Lord had brought him out of the prison. And he said, go shew these things unto James and to the brethren, and he departed, and went into another place. God can and will deliver out of prison but we must have faith.

Prayer can cast out demons. The disciple had cast out many demons but now they met a demon that they were not able to cast out. Matthew 17:14-21 And when they were come to the multitude, there came to Him a certain man, kneeling down to Him, and saying Lord, have mercy on my son: for he is lunatick, and sore vexed: for ofttimes he falleth into fire, and oft into the water. And I brought him to thy disciples, and they could not cure him. Then Jesus answered and said, O faithless and perverse generation, how long shall I be with you? How long shall I suffer you? Bring him hither to me. And Jesus rebuked the devil; and he departed out of him: and the child was cured from that very hour. Then came the disciples to Jesus apart, and said, why could not we cast him out? And Jesus said unto them, because of your unbelief: for verily I say unto you. If ye have faith as a grain of mustard see, ye shall say unto this mountain, Remove hence to yonder place; and it shall remove; and nothing shall be impossible unto you. Howbeit this kind goeth not out but by prayer and fasting.

Prayer can hold back the judgment of God. Exodus 33:7-17 And Moses took the tabernacle, and pitched it without the camp, afar off from the camp and called it the Tabernacle of the congregation. And it came to pass, that everyone which sought the Lord went out unto the tabernacle of the congregation, which was without the camp. And it came to pass, when Moses went out unto unto the tabernacle, that all the people rose up and stood every man at his tent door, and looked after Moses, until he was gone into the tabernacle, And it came to pass, as Moses entered into the tabernacle, cloudy pillar descended, and stood at the door of the tabernacle, and the Lord talked with Moses. And all the people saw the cloudy pillar stand at the tabernacle door: and all the people rose up and worshipped, every man in his tent door. And the Lord spake unto Moses face to face, as a man speaketh unto his friend. And he turned again into the camp, but his servant Joshua, the son of Nun, a young man, departed not out of the tabernacle. And Moses said unto the Lord, see, thou sayest unto me. Bring up this people: and thou hast not let me know whom thou wilt send with me. Yet thou hast said, I know thee by name, and thou hast also found grace in my sight. Now therefore, I pray thee, if I have found grace in thy sight, show me now thy way, that I may know thee, that I may find grace in thy sight: and consider that this nation is thy people. And he said, my presence shall go with thee, and I will give thee rest. And he said unto him; if thy presence go not with me, carry us not up hence. For wherein shall it be known here that I and thy people found grace in thy sight? Is it not in that you go with us? So shall we be separated, I and thy people, from all the people that are upon the face of the earth And the Lord said unto Moses. I will do this thing also that thou hast spoken: for you have found grace in my sight, and I know thee my name.

Prayer will open the barren womb. Hannah prayer for a child and God answered her. I Samuel 1:1-28 Now there was a certain man of Ramathaim-zophim, of mount Ephraim, and his name was Elkanah, the son of Jeroham, the son of Elihu, the son of Tohu the son of Zuph, an Ephrathite: And he had two wives, the name of the one was Hannah, and the name of the other was Peninnah and Peninnah had children, but Hannah had no children. And this man went up out of his city yearly to worship and to sacrifice unto the Lord of hosts in Shiloh and the two sons of Eli, Hophni and Phinehas, the priests of the Lord, were there. And when the time was that Elkanah offered, he gave to Peninnah his wife; and to all her sons and daughters a portion. But unto Hannah he gave a worthy portion; for he loved Hannah: but the Lord had shut up her womb. And her adversary also provoked her sore, for to make her fret, because the Lord had shut up her womb? And as he did so year by year, when she went up to the house of the Lord, so she provoked her; therefore she wept, and did not eat. Then said Elkanah her husband to her, Hannah, why weepest thou? And why eatest thou not? And why is thy heart grieved? Am I better to thee than ten sons? So Hannah rose up after they had eaten in Shiloh, and after they had drunk. Now Eli the priest sat upon a seat by a post of the temple of the Lord. And she was in bitterness of soul, and prayed unto the Lord, and wept sore. And she vowed a vow, and said, O Lord of hosts, if thou wilt indeed look on the affliction of thine handmaid, and remember me, and not forget thine handmaid, but wilt give unto thine handmaid a man child, then, I will give him unto the Lord all the days of his life, and there shall no razor come upon his head. And it came to pass, as she continued praying before the Lord, that Eli marked her mouth. Now Hannah, she spake in her heart; only her lips moved, but her voice was not heard; therefore Eli thought she had been drunken. And Eli said unto her, How long wilt thou be drunken? Put away thy wine from thee. And Hannah answered and said, No, my lord, I am a woman of a sorrowful spirit: I have drunk neither wine nor strong drink, but have poured out my soul before the Lord. Count not thine handmaid for a daughter of Belial; for out of the abundance of my complaint and grief have I spoken hitherto. Then Eli answered and said, go in peace: and the God of Israel grants thee thy petition that thou hast asked of Him. And she said, let thine handmaid find grace in thy sight. So the woman went her way, and did eat, and her countenance was no more sad. And they rose up in the morning early, and worshipped before before the Lord, and returned, and came to their house to Ramah: and Elkanah knew Hannah his wife; and the Lord remembered her. Wherefore it came to pass when the time was come about after Hannah had conceived, that she bare a son, and called his name Samuel, saying I have asked him of the Lord.

Prayer can cause the sick to be healed. James 5:13-16 Is any among you afflicted? Let him pray. Is any merry? Let him sing psalms. Is any sick among you? Let him call for the elders of the church; and let them pray over him, anointing him with oil in the name of the Lord. And the prayer of faith shall save the sick, and the Lord shall raise him up; and if he has committed sins they shall be forgiven him. Confess your faults one to another, and pray one for another, that ye may be healed. The effectual fervent prayer of a righteous man availeth much.

Prayer can withhold rain and cause the heaven to give rain after it is withheld. James 5:17-18 Elias was a man subject to like passions as we are, and he prayed earnestly that it might not rain; and it rained not on the earth by the space of three years and six months. And he prayed again, and the heaven gave rain, and the earth brought forth her fruit.

In order for prayer to work, there are other things that enhance prayer like prayer and forgiveness go hand and hand. Mark 11:24-25 Therefore I say unto you, what things soever ye desire, when ye pray, believe that ye receive them, and ye shall have them. And when ye stand praying, forgive, if ye have ought against any; that your Father also which is in heaven may forgive you your trespasses. But if ye do not forgive, neither will your Father which is in heaven forgive your trespasses.

Pray without ceasing 2 Timothy 1:3 I thank God, whom I serve from my forefathers with pure conscience, that without ceasing I have remembrance of thee in my prayers night and day. Colossians 1:9 For this cause we also, since the day we heard it do not cease to pray for you and to desire that ye might be filled with the knowledge of His will in all wisdom and spiritual understanding.

Obedience is always importance in prayer. Ananias obeys the Lord and victory can. Acts 9:1-20 And Saul, yet breathing out threatenings and slaughter against the disciples of the Lord, went unto the high priest. And desired of him letters to Damascus to the synagogues, that if he found any of this way, whether they were men or women, he might bring them bound unto Jerusalem. And as he journeyed, he came near Damascus: and suddenly there shined round about him a light from heaven: And he fell to the earth, and heard a voice saying unto him, Saul, Saul, why persecutes thou me? And he said, who art thou Lord? And the Lord said I am Jesus whom thou persecute: It is hard for thee to kick against the pricks. And he trembling and astonished said, Lord. What wilt thou have me to do? And the Lord said unto him, Arise, and go into the city, and it shall be told thee what thou must do. And the men which journeyed with him stood speechless, hearing a voice but seeing no man. And Saul arose from the earth; and when his eyes were opened, he saw no man; but they led him by the hand, and brought him into Damascus. And he was three days without sight, and neither did eat nor drink. And there was a certain disciple at Damascus, named Ananias; and to him said the Lord in a vision, Ananias. And he said, Behold, I am here Lord. And the Lord said unto him, Arise, and go into the street which is called Straight, and enquire in the house of Judas for one called Saul of Tarsus: for, behold, he prayeth. And hath seen in a vision a man named Ananias coming in, and putting his hand on him, that he might receive his sight. Then Ananias answered, Lord, I have heard; by many of this man, how much evil he hath done to thy saints at Jerusalem; and here he hath authority from the chief priests to bind all that call on thy name. But the Lord said unto him, go thy way: for he is a chosen vessel unto me, to bear my name before the Gentiles, and kings, and the children of Israel; for I will shew him how great things he must suffer for my name's sake. And Ananias went his way, and entered into the house; and putting his hands on him said, Brother Saul, the Lord, even Jesus, that appeared unto thee in the way as thou camest, hath sent me, that thou mightiest receive thy sight, and be filled with the Holy Ghost. And immediately there fell from his eyes as it had been scales: and he received sight forthwith, and rose, and was baptized. And when he had received meat, he was strengthened. Then was Saul certain days with the disciples which were at Damascus. And straightway he preached Christ in the synagogues, that he is the Son of God.

Prayer and Faith. James 1:5-8 If any of you lack wisdom, let him ask of God, that giveth to all men liberally, and upbraideth not; and it shall be given him. But let him ask in faith, nothing wavering. For he that wavereth is like a wave of the sea driven with the wind and tossed. For let not that man think that he shall receive any thing of the Lord. A double minded man is unstable in all his way.

There are hindrances to prayer. We need to remove hinder to make prayer effectively.

Sin in our lives is a big hinder to prayer. Psalm 66:18 If I regard iniquity in my heart the Lord will not hear me: Isaiah 59:1-2 Behold the Lord's hand is not shortened, that it cannot save, neither his ear heavy that it cannot hear. But your iniquities have separated between you and you God, and your sins have hid his face from you, that he will not hear. Romans 6:23 for the wages of sin is death; but the gift of God is eternal life through Jesus Christ our Lord. Romans 6:1-**2** what shall we say then? Shall we continue in sin, that grace may abound? God forbid, how shall we, that are dead to sin, live any longer therein?

Improper Husband and wife relationship—I Peter 3:7 Likewise, ye husbands, dwell with them according to knowledge, giving honour unto the wife, as unto the weaker vessel, and as being heirs together of the grace of life; that your prayers be not hindered. Malachi 2:14-17 Yet ye say, Wherefore? Because the Lord hath been witness between thee and the wife of thy youth, against whom thou hast dealt treacherously; yet is she thy companion, and the wife of thy covenant. And did not he make one? Yet had he the residue of the spirit. And wherefore one? That he might seek a godly seed. Therefore take heed to your spirit, and let no one deal treacherously against the wife of his youth, For the Lord, the God of Israel, saith that he hateth putting away; for one covereth, violence with his garment, saith the Lord of hosts; therefore take heed to your spirit, that ye deal not treacherously. Ye have wearied the Lord with your words. Yet ye say, wherein have we wearied him? When ye say, everyone that doeth evil is good in the sight of the Lord, and he delighteth in them, or, where is the God of judgment?

Double mind is another hinder to prayer-James 1:5-8 If any of you lack wisdom, let him ask of God, that giveth to all men liberally, and upbraideth not; and it shall be given him. But let him ask in faith, nothing wavereth. For he that wavereth is like a wave of the sea driven with the wind and tossed. For let not that man thinks he shall receive anything of the Lord. A double minded man is unstable in all his ways.

Unbelief—we can overcome unbelief through the word of God. Doubt is one of the biggest hindrances to our prayer life. Mark 9:23 Jesus said unto him, If thou canst believe, all things are possible to him that believeth. Mark 11:22-24 And Jesus answering saith unto them, Have faith in God. For verily I say unto you. That whosoever shall say unto this mountain, Be thou removed, and be thou cast into the sea; and shall not doubt in his heart, but shall believe that those things which he saith shall come to pass; he shall have whatsoever he saith. Therefore I say unto you what things soever ye desire, when ye pray, believe that ye receive them, and ye shall have them. Hebrews 11:6 But without faith it is impossible to please Him: for he that cometh to God must believe that He is, and that He is a rewarder of them that diligently seek Him.

Not asking according to the will of God. James 4:1-4 From whence come wars and fightings among you? Come they not hence, even of your lusts that war in your members? Ye lust, and have not: ye kill and desire to have, and cannot obtain: ye fight and war, yet ye have not, because ye ask not. Ye ask, and receive not, because ye ask amiss, that ye may consume it upon your lusts. Ye adulterers and adulteresses, know ye not that the friendship of the world is enmity with God? Whosoever therefore will be a friend of the world is the enemy of God. I John 5:14-15 And this is the confidence that we have in Him, that, if we ask anything according to His will, He heareth us: And if we know that He hear us, whatsoever we ask, we know that we have the petitions that we desired of Him. Romans 8:26-27

Likewise the Spirit also helpeth our infirmities: for we know not what we should pray for as we ought: but the Spirit itself maketh intercession for us with groanings which cannot be uttered. And He that searcheth the hearts knoweth what is the mind of the Spirit, because He maketh intercession for the saints according to the will of God.

Unforgiveness—We must forgive and forgive from our hearts in order for prayer to be effectively. Matthew 18:21-38 Then came Peter to Him, and said, Lord, how oft shall my brother sin against me, and I forgive him? Till seven times? Jesus saith unto him, I say not unto thee, until seven times: but until seventy times seven. Therefore is kingdom of heaven likened unto a certain king, which would take account of his servants. And when he had begun to reckon, one was brought unto him, which owed him ten thousand talents. But forasmuch as he had not to pay, his lord commanded him to be sold; and his wife, and children and all that he had, and payment to be made. The servant therefore fell down, and worshipped him, saying, Lord, have patience with me, and I will pay thee all. Then the lord of that servant was moved with compassion and loosed him, and forgave him the debt. But the same servant went out, and found one of his fellowservants, which owed him an hundred pence; and he laid hands on him, and took him by the throat, saying. Pay me that thou owest. And his fellowservant fell down at his feet, and besought him, saying. Have patience with me, and I will pay thee all. And he would not; but went and cast him into prison, till he should pay the debt. So when his fellowservants saw what was done, they were very sorry, and came and told unto their lord all that was done. Then his lord, after that he had called him, said unto him, O thou wicked servant. I forgave thee all that debt, because thou desiredst me. Shouldest not thou also have had compassion on thy fellowservant, even as I had pity on thee? And his lord was wroth, and delivered him to the tormentors, till he should pay all that was due unto him. So likewise shall my heavenly Father do also unto you, if ye from your hearts forgive not everyone his brother their trespasses. Mark 11:23-26 For verily I say unto you, that whosoever shall say unto this mountain, be thou removed, and be thou cast into the sea; and shall not doubt in his heart, but shall believe that those things which he saith shall come to pass; he shall have whatsoever he saith. Therefore I say unto you, what things soever ye desire, when ye pray. Believe that ye receive them and ye shall have them. And when ye stand praying, forgive, if ye have ought against any: that your Father also which is in heaven may forgive you your trespasses. But if ye do not forgive, neither will your Father which is in heaven forgive your trespasses.

Improper motive-We don't need to pray to be seen, use vain repetition and trying to be heard by other. Our prayer is to the Lord and is not to people. Matthew 6:5-8 And when thou prayest, thou shalt not be as the hypocrites are, for they love to pray standing in the synagogues and in the corners of the streets that they may be seen of men. Verily I say unto you, they have their reward. But thou, when thou prayest, enter into thy closet, and when thou hast shut thy door pray to thy Father which is in secret; and thy Father which seeth in secret shall reward thee openly. But ye pray, use not vain repetitions, as the heathen do, for they think that they shall be heard for their much speaking. Be not ye therefore like unto them, for your Father knoweth what things ye have need of, before ye ask him.

Lack of power with God. Acts 1:8 But ye shall receive power, after that the Holy Ghost is come upon you, and ye shall be witnesses unto me both in Jerusalem, and in all Judaea, and in Samaria, and unto the uttermost part of the earth. Ephesians 3:20 Now unto Him that is able to do exceeding abundantly above all that we ask or think, according to the power that worketh in us. Ephesians 6:10 Finally, my brethren, be strong in the Lord and in the power of His might.

Failure to use the Name of Jesus. John 14:12-14 Verily, verily, I say unto you, He that believeth on me, the works that I do shall he do also; and greater works than these shall he do; because I go unto my Father. And whatsoever ye shall ask in my name, that will I do that the Father may be glorified in the Son. If ye shall ask any thing in my name, I will do it.

Unthankfulness-Ephesians 5:4 Neither filthiness, nor foolish talking, nor jesting, which are not convenient; but rather giving of thanks. Ephesians 5:20 Giving thanks always for all things unto God and the Father in the name of our Lord Jesus Christ. Philippians 4:6 Be careful for nothing, but in everything by prayer and supplication with thanksgiving let your requests be made known unto God.

Disobedience to God's Word. I John 3:19-22 And hereby we know that we are of the truth, and shall assure our hearts before Him. For if our heart condemn us, God is greater than our heart, and knoweth all things. Beloved, if our heart condemn us not, then have we confidence toward God. And whatsoever we ask, we receive of Him, because we keep His commandments, and do those things that are pleasing in His sight. And this is His commandment, That we should believe on the name of His son Jesus Christ, and love one another.

Prayer change things but I believe the most importance thing about prayer is that it change us. Pray can change our spirit, attitude, can give us a whole new look at a situation especially when prayer is joined with the

Word of God. Luke 18:9-14 And He spake this parable unto certain which trusted in themselves that they were righteous, and despised other. Two men went up into the temple to pray: the one a Pharisee, and the other a publican. The Pharisee stood and prayed thus with himself, God, I thank thee, that I am not as other men are, extortioners, unjust, adulterers, or even as this publican. I fast twice a week; I give tithes of all that I possess. And the publican, standing afar off, would not lift up so much as his eyes unto heaven, but smote upon his breast, saying, God be merciful to me a sinner. I tell you, this man went down to his house justified rather than the other; for everyone that exalteth himself; shall be abased; and he that humbleth himself shall be exalted. The publican went away a change man, justified before the Lord because he humbled himself. Pray change us.

Peter life was change through prayer. Acts 10:1-23 There was a certain man in Caesarea called Cornelius, a centurion of the band called the Italian band. A devout man, and one that feared God with all his house, which gave much alms to the people, and prayed to God always. He saw in a vision evidently about the ninth hour of the day an angel of God coming in to him and saying unto him, Cornelius. And when he looked on him, he was afraid, and said, what is it, Lord? And he said unto him, thy prayers and thine alms are come up for a memorial before God. And now send men to Joppa, and call for one Simon, whose surname is Peter. He lodgeth with one Simon a tanner, whose house is by the sea side he shall tell thee what thou oughtest to do. And when the angel which spake unto Cornelius was departed, he called two of his household servants, and a devout soldier of them, that waited on him continually; and when he had declared all these things unto them, he sent them to Joppa. On the morrow, as they went on their journey, and drew nigh unto the city, Peter went up upon the housetop to pray about the sixth hour. And he became very hungry, and would have eaten; but while they made ready he fell into a trance. And saw heaven opened, and a certain vessel descending unto him, as it had been a great sheet knit at the four corners, and let down to the earth. Wherein were all manner of four footed beasts of the earth, and wild beasts, and creeping things and fowls of the air. And there came a voice to him, rise, Peter, kill, and eat. But Peter said, not so, Lord; I have never eaten anything that is common or unclean. And the voice spake unto him again the second time, what God hath cleansed, that call not thou common. This was done thrice: and the vessel was received up again into heaven. Now while Peter doubted in himself what this vision which he had seen should mean, behold, the men which were sent from Cornelius had made enquiry for Simon's house, and stood before the gate. And called, and asked whether Simon which was surnamed Peter, were lodged there. Where Peter thought on the vision, the spirit said unto him, behold, three men seek thee. Arise therefore, and get thee down, and go with them, doubting nothing for I have sent them. Then Peter went down to the men who were sent unto him from Cornelius, and said, Behold, I am he whom ye seek: what is the cause wherefore ye are come? And they said, Cornelius the centurion, a just man, and one that feareth God, and of good report among all the nation of the Jews, was warned from God by a holy angel to send for thee into his house, and to hear words of thee. Then called he them in, and lodged them. And on the morrow Peter went away with them, and certain brethren from Joppa accompanied him.

After Job prayed he also was change and accepts by God. Job 42:7-10 And it was so, that after the Lord had spoken these words unto Job, the Lord said to Eliphaz the Temanite, My wrath is kindled against thee, and against thy two friends; for ye have not spoken of me the thing that is right, as my servant Job hath. Therefore take unto now seven bullocks and seven rams, and go to my servant Job, and offer up for yourselves a burnt offering; and my servant Job shall pray for you; for him will I accept: lest I deal with you after your folly, in that ye have not spoken of me the thing which is right, like my servant Job. So Eliphaz theTemanite and Bildad the Shuhite and Zophar the Naamathite went; and did according as the Lord commanded them: the Lord also accept Job. And the Lord turned the captivity of Job, when he prayed for his friends; also the Lord gave Job twice as much as he had before.

When Jonah cried out to the Lord it changes his life. Jonah 2:1-10 Then Jonah prayed unto the Lord his God out of the fish's belly. And said, I cried by reason of mine affliction unto the Lord, and he heard me; out of the belly of hell cried I, and thou heardest my voice. For thou hadst cast me into the deep, in the midst of the seas; and the floods compassed me about; all thy billows and thy waves passed over me. Then I said, I am cast out of thy sight; yet I will look again toward the holy temple. The waters compassed me about, even to the soul: the depth closed me round about; the weeds were wrapped about my head. I went down to the bottoms of the mountains; the earth with her bars was about me forever; yet hast thou brought up my life from corruption, O Lord my God. When my soul fainted within me I remembered the Lord: and my prayer came in unto thee, into thine holy temple. They that observe lying vanities forsake their own mercy. But I will sacrifice unto thee with the voice of thanksgiving; I will pay that I have vowed. Salvation is of the Lord. And the Lord Spake unto the fish, and it vomited out Jonah upon the dry land.

Prayer can cause God to repent (to change his mind). Exodus 32:7-14 And the Lord said unto Moses, go, get down; for thy people, which thou broughtest out of the land of Egypt, have corrupted themselves; They have turned aside quickly out of the way which I have commanded them: they have made them a molten calf, and have worshipped it, and have sacrificed thereunto, and said, These be thy gods, O Israel, which have brought thee up out of the land of Egypt. And the Lord said unto Moses, I have seen this people, and, behold, it is a stiffnecked people: Now therefore let me alone, that my wrath may hot again them, and that I may consume them; and I will make of thee a great nation. And Moses besought the Lord his God, and said, Lord, why doth thy wrath wax hot against thy people, which thou hast brought forth out of the land of Egypt with great power, and with a mighty hand? Wherefore should the Egyptians speak, and say, for mischief did he bring them out, to slay them in the mountains, and to consume them from the face of the earth? Turn from thy fierce wrath, and repent of this evil against thy people. Remember Abraham, Isaac, and Israel, thy servants, to whom thou swarest by thine own self, and saidst unto them, I will multiply your seed as the stars of heaven, and all this land that I have spoken of will I give unto your seed, and they shall inherit it forever. And the Lord repented of the evil which He thought to do his people.

Prayer can cause change in the life of other, when we pray for them. James 5:14-15 Is any sick among you? Let him call for the elders of the church; and let them pray over him, anointing him with oil in the name of the Lord. And the prayer of faith shall save the sick, and the Lord shall raise him up, and if he has committed sins, they shall be forgiven him. Confess your faults one to another, and pray one for another, that ye may be healed. The effectual fervent prayer of a righteous man availeth much.

Pray for those who despitefully use you. Matthew 5:44-48 But I say unto you, Love your enemies, bless them that curse you, do good to them that hate you, and pray for them which despitefully use you, and persecute you. That you may be the children of your Father which is in heaven, for he maketh His sun to rise on the evil and on the good, and sendeth rain on the just and on the unjust. For if ye love them which love you, what reward have ye? Do not even the publicans the same? And if ye salute your brethren only? What do ye more than others? Do not even publicans so? Be ye therefore perfect, even as your Father which is in heaven is perfect.

Never! Never! Give up in prayer.

YES, I CAN FAST. Matthew 6:16-18 Moreover when ye fast, be not, as the hypocrites, of a sad countenance; for they disfigure their faces, that they may appear unto men to fast. Verily I say unto you, they have their reward. But thou, when thou fastest, anoint thine head, and wash their face; That thou appear not unto men to fast, but unto thy Father which is in secret, and thy Father which seeth in secret, shall reward thee openly. Matthew 9:14-15 Then came to Him the disciples of John, saying why do we and the Pharisees fast oft, but thy disciples fast not? And Jesus said unto them, Can the children of the bridechamber mourn, as long as the bridegroom is with them? But the days will come, when the bridegroom shall be taken from them, and then shall they fast.

The first sin took place when Eve ate of the forbidden from the tree that was in the midst of the garden. Genesis 3:6 And when the woman saw that the tree was good for food, and that it was pleasant to the eye and a tree to be desired to make one wise, she took of the fruit thereof, and did eat, and gave also unto her husband with her; and he did eat.

Immortal and fullness of bread was sin of Sodom and Gomorrah. Ezekiel 16:49 Behold, this was the iniquity of thy sister Sodom, pride, fullness of bread, and abundance of idleness was in her and in her daughters, neither did she strengthen the hand of the poor and needy.

Fasting is simply going without food or water and food. Fasting come from the Hebrew word tsuwm meaning to cover the mouth. The Greek word for fasting is nestis which not eating, to abstain from food. Fasting is doing without food for a spiritual purpose and strength. Zechariah 7:5 Speak unto all the people of the land, and to the priests, saying, when ye fasted and mourned in the fifth and seventh month, even those seventy years, did ye at all fast unto me, even to me. We should fast unto the Lord and not until men.

There are three type of fasting found in the Bible. People call them the normal fast, absolute fast and partial fast.

Normal Fast is when we abstain from food, but drink water. Matthew 4:1-2 Then was Jesus led up of the Spirit into the wilderness to be tempted of the devil. And when He had fasted forty days and forty nights, He was afterward a hungered. Luke 4:1-2 And Jesus being full of the Holy Ghost returned from Jordan, and was led by the Spirit into the wilderness. Being forty days tempted of the devil. And in those days He eats nothing: and when they were ended, He afterward hungered.

Absolute Fast is abstaining from water and food. For our healthy, it may not be good to go without water for more than three days. Acts 9:1-9 And Saul, yet breathing out threatenings and slaughter against the disciples of the Lord, went unto the high priest. And desired of him letters to

Damascus to the synagogues, that if he found any of this way, whether they were men or women, he might bring them bound unto Jerusalem. And as he journeyed, he came near Damascus: and suddenly there shined round about him a light from heaven: And he fell to the earth, and heard a voice saying unto him, Saul, Saul, why persecutes thou me? And he said, who art thou, Lord? And the Lord said, I am Jesus whom thou persecutest. It is hard for thee to kick against the pricks. And he trembling and astonished said, Lord, what wilt thou have me to do? And the Lord said unto him, Arise, and go into the city, and it shall be told thee what thou must do. And the men which journeyed with him stood speechless, hearing a voice, but seeing no man. And Saul arose from the earth; and when his eyes were opened, he saw no man: but they led him by the hand, and brought him into Damascus. And he was three days without sight, and neither did eat nor drink. Ezra 10:6 Then Ezra rose up from before the house of God, and went into the chamber of Johanan the son of Eliashib; and when he came thither, he did eat no bread, nor drink water: for he mourned because of the transgression of them that had been carried away.

Partial Fast we abstain from some food and may eat fruits and vegetables. Daniel 1:8-15 But Daniel purposed in his heart that he would not defile himself with the portion of the King's meat, nor with the wine which he drank, therefore he requested of the prince of the eunuchs that he might not defile himself. Now God had brought Daniel into favour and tender love with the prince of the eunuchs. And the prince of the eunuchs said unto Daniel, I fear my lord the king, who hath appointed your meat and your drink; for why should he see your faces worse liking than the children which are of your sort? Then shall ye make me endanger my head to the king. Then said Daniel to Melzar, whom the prince of the eunuchs had set over Daniel, Hananiah, Mishael and Azariah. Prove thy servants, I beseech thee, ten days, and let them give us pulse to eat, and water to drink. Then let our countenances be looked upon before thee, and the countenance of the children that eat of the portion of the king's meat, and as thou seest, deal with thy servants. So he consented to them in this matter, and proved them ten days. And at the end of ten days their countenances appeared fairer and fatter in flesh than all the children which did eat the portion of the king's meat. Daniel 10:2-3 In those days I Daniel was mourning three full weeks. I ate no pleasant bread, neither came flesh nor wine in my mouth, neither did I anoint myself at all, till three whole weeks were fulfilled.

David fasted. 2 Samuel 12:-14-23 Howbeit, because by this deed thou hast given great occasion to the enemies of the Lord to blaspheme, the child also that is born unto thee shall surely die. And Nathan departed unto his house. And the Lord struck the child that Uriah's wife bare unto David, and it was very sick. David therefore besought God for the child, and David fasted, and went in and lay all night upon the earth. And the elders of his house arose, and went to him, to raise him up from the earth: but he would not, neither did he eat bread with them. And it came to pass on the seventh day, that the child died. And the servants of David feared to tell him that the child dead. For they said, Behold, while the child was yet alive, we spake unto him, and he would not hearken unto our voice how will he then vex himself, if we tell him that the child is dead? But when David saw that his servants whispered, David perceived that the child was dead: therefore David said unto his servants, Is the child dead? And they said, He is dead. Then David arose from the earth, and washed, and anointed himself, and changed his apparel, and came into the house of the Lord; and worshipped: then he came to his own house; and when he required, they set bread before him, and he did eat. Then said his servants unto him, what thing is this that thou hast done? Thou didst fast and weep for the child, while it was alive; but when the child was dead, thou didst rise and eat bread. And he said, while the child was yet alive. I fasted and wept: for I said, who can tell whether God will be gracious to me, that the child may live? But now he is dead, wherefore should I fast? Can I bring him back again? I shall go to him, but he shall not return to me.

Esther, her maids, and Jews fasted. Esther 4:16-5:1-3 Go, gather together all the Jews that are present in Shushan, and fast ye for me, and neither eat nor drink three days, night or day: I also and my maidens will fast likewise; and so will I go in unto the kings, which is not according to the law, and if I perish, I perish. So Mordecai went his way, and did according to all that Esther has commanded him. Now it came to pass on the third day, that Esther put on her royal apparel, and stood in the inner court of the king's house, over against the king's house: and the king sat upon his royal throne in the royal house, over against the gate of the house. And it was so, when the king saw Esther the queen standing in the court, that she obtained favour in his sight and the king held out to Esther the golden sceptre that was in his hand. So Esther drew near, and touched the top of the sceptre. Then said the king unto her, what wilt thou Queen Esther? And what is thy request? It shall be even given thee to the half of the kingdom.

Moses fasted. Deuteronomy 9:9 When I was gone up into the mount to receive the tables of stone, even the tables of the covenant which the Lord made with you, then I abode in the mount forty days and forty nights, I neither did eat bread nor drink water.

There are things we should and shouldn't do while we are fasting. Isaiah 58:3-12 Wherefore have we fasted, say they, and thou seest not? Wherefore have we afflicted our soul, and thou takest no knowledge? Behold, in the day of your fast ye find pleasure, and exact all your labours. Behold, ye fast for strife and debate, and to smite with the fist of wickedness. Ye shall not fast as ye do this day, to make your voice to be heard on high. Is it such a fast that I have chosen? A day for a man to afflict his soul? Is it to bow down his head as a bulrush, and to spread sackcloth and ashes under him? Wilt thou call this a fast, and acceptable day to the Lord? Is not this the fast that I have chosen? To loose the bands of wickedness, to undo the heavy burden, and to let the oppressed go free, and that ye break every yoke? Is it not to deal thy bread to the hungry, and that thou bring the poor that are cast out to thy house? When thou seest the naked, that thou cover him, and that thou hide not thyself from thine own flesh? Then shall thy light break forth as the morning, and thine health shall spring forth speedily; and thy righteousness shall go before thee: the glory of the Lord shall be thy **reward**. Then shalt thou call, and the Lord, shall answer: thou shalt cry and he shall say, here I am if thou take away from the midst of thee the yoke, the putting forth of the finger, and speaking vanity. And if thou draw out they soul to the hungry, and satisfy the afflicted soul; then shall thy light rise in obscurity and thy darkness be as the noonday. And the Lord shall guide thee continually, and satisfy thy soul in drought, and make fat thy bones, and thou shalt be like a watered garden, and like a spring of water, whose waters fail not. And they that shall be of thee shall build the old waste places; thou shalt raise up the foundations of many generations; and thou shall be called. The repairer of the breach, the restorer of paths to dwell in.

Things we should do while we are fasting.

We should loose the bands of the wickedness. Isaiah 58:6 Is not this the fast that I have chosen? To loose the bands of wickedness. We are to separate ourselves from anything that is wrong in our life.

We are to undo heavy burden. Isaiah 58:6 Is not this the fast that I have chosen? To loose the bands of the wickedness, to undo the heavy burdens. We should let go of physically and spiritually burden. We should cast all our cares upon the Lord, because He cares for us and spent as much time as possible in prayer.

Let the oppressed go free. Isaiah 58:6 Is not this the fast that I have chosen? To let the oppressed go free. Let this be a day of forgiving other their trespasses, and offenses, and treat other with kindness.

Break every yoke. Isaiah 58:6 Is not this the fast that I have chosen? That ye break every yoke? Hebrews 12:1 Wherefore seeing we also are compassed about with so great a cloud of witnesses, let us lay aside every weight, and the sin which doth so easily beset us, and let us run with patience the race that is set before us.

Deal thy bread to the hungry and that thou bring the poor that are cast out to thy house. Psalm 41:1-3 Blessed is he that considereth the poor: the Lord will deliver him in time of trouble. The Lord will preserve him, and keep him alive; and he shall be blessed upon the earth: and thou wilt not deliver him unto the will of his enemies. The Lord will strengthen him upon the bed of languishing: thou wilt make all his bed in his sickness.

When thou seest the naked, that thou cover him. Take care of physically and spiritually needs Matthew 25:31-46 When the Son of Man shall come in the glory, and all the holy angels with him, and then shall he sit upon the throne of His glory. And before Him shall be gathered all nations: and He shall separate them one from another, as a shepherd divideth His sheep from the goats: And He shall set the sheep on His right hand, but the goats on the left. Then shall the King say unto them on His right hand, Come, ye blessed of my Father, inherit the kingdom prepared for you from the foundation of the world. For I was a hungred, and ye gave me meat. I was thirsty, and ye gave me drink. I was a stranger, and ye took me in: Naked, and ye clothed me. I was sick, and ye visited me: I was in prison, and ye came unto me. Then shall the righteous answer Him, saying, Lord. When saw we thee a hungred, and fed thee? Or thirsty, and gave thee drink? When saw we thee a stranger, and took thee in? or naked, and clothed thee? Or when saw we thee sick, or in prison, and came unto thee? And the King shall answer and say unto them, verily I say unto you, in as much as ye have done it unto one of the least of these my brethren, ye have done it unto me. Then shall he say also unto them on the left hand, Depart from me, ye cursed, into everlasting fire, prepared for the devil and his angels. For I was an hungred, and ye gave me no meat: I was thirsty, and ye gave me no drink: I was a stranger, and ye took me not in: naked, and ye clothed me not: sick, and in prison, and ye visited me not. Then shall they also answer Him, saying, Lord when saw we thee a hungred, or athirst, or a stranger, or naked, or sick, or in prison, and did not minister unto thee? Then shall He answer them, saying, verily I say unto you, inasmuch as ye did it not to one of the least of these, ye did it not to me. And these shall go away into everlasting punishment: but the righteous into life eternal.

Hide not thyself from thine own flesh. Saint of God needs to keep unity in the body of Christ. Brotherhood need to be restored. Matthew 5:23-24

Therefore if thou bring thy gift to the altar, and there rememberest that thy brother hath ought against thee; Leave there thy gift before the altar, and go thy way, first be reconciled to thy brother, and then come and offer thy gift.

Anoint thine head, and wash thy face. We are to go forth as on other days, not appear unto men but unto the Lord. Matthew 6:16-18 Moreover when ye fast, be not, as the hypocrites, of a sad countenance: for they disfigure their faces, that they may appear unto men to fast. Verily I say unto you, they have their reward. But anoint thine head, and wash thy face; that thou appear not unto men to fast, but unto thy Father which is in secret: and thy Father, which seeth in secret, shall reward thee openly.

Things we should not do when we are fasting.

Find pleasure and exact all your labours. Isaiah 58:3 Behold, in the day of your fast ye find pleasure, and exact all your labours (oppress all your labourers). We should lay aside pleasure and business as possible to obtain the most from our fast. Spend as much time as possible in prayer and study of the word of God.

Fasting for strife and debate. Fasting to exalt ourselves should not be done. Philippians 2:2-3 Fulfill ye my joy, that ye be likeminded, having the same love, being of one accord, of one mind. Let nothing be done through strife or vainglory; but in lowliness of mind let each esteems other better than themselves.

Smite with the fist of wickedness. Don't persist in hypocritical ways. Give up every sin. Romans 6:1-2 What shall we say then? Shall we continue in sin, that grace may abound? God forbid. How shall we, that are dead to sin, live any longer therein?

Be of a sad countenance. Matthew 6:16 Moreover when ye fast, be not, as the hypocrites, of a sad countenance, for they disfigure their face, that they may appear unto men to fast. Verily I say unto you. They have their reward.

As we fast as God has command us. The promises of God will be fulfill in our life. There are sixteen promises and blessing when we fast as God has command us.

1. Then shall thy light break forth as the morning.
2. Thine health shall spring forth speedily
3. Thy righteousness shall go before thee.
4. The glory of the Lord shall be thy reward.
5. Then shalt thou call, and the Lord shall answer.
6. Thou shalt cry: and He shall say, here I am.
7. Then shalt thy light arise in obscurity.
8. Thy darkness shall be as the moon day.
9. The Lord shall guide thee continually.
10. The Lord shall satisfy thy soul in drought.
11. The Lord shall make fat thy bone
12. Thou shalt be like a watered garden.
13. Thou shalt be like a spring of water, whose water fail not.
14. They that shall be of thee shall build the old waste places.
15. Thou shalt raise up the foundations of many generations.
16. Thou shalt be called, the repairer of the breach, the restorer of paths to dwell in.

And let not forget it give us power over the devil. Mathew 17:18-21 And Jesus rebuked the devil; and he departed out of him: and the child was cured from that very hour. Then came the disciples to Jesus apart, and said, why could not we cast him out? And Jesus said unto them, Because of your unbelief: for verily I say unto you, if ye have faith as a grain of mustard seed, ye shall say unto this mountain, Remove hence to yonder place; and it shall remove, and nothing shall be impossible unto you. Howbeit this kind goeth not out but by prayer and fasting.

When your pastor call for a time of fasting always obey. Hebrews 13:17 Obey them that have the rule over you, and submit yourselves: for they watch for your souls, as they that must give account, that they may do it with joy, and not with grief. For that is unprofitable for you.

Commit yourself to fast on a regular basis.

Whenever is possible go on extend fast for more than one day.

I was always taught to take the same number of days of fasting to break a fast, if you fasted for three days you need to take three day to break your fast to return to normal eating. A fast should break with light food, juices and fruit. This will help prevent stomach upset.

YES, **I CAN ATTEND THE HOUSE OF THE LORD.** To be successful as a child of God, we need the house of God. Deuteronomy 12:5-7 But unto the place which the Lord your God shall choose out of all your tribes to put His name there, even unto his habitation shall ye seek, and thither thou shall come. And thither ye shall bring your burnt offerings, and your sacrifices, and your tithes, and heave offerings of your hands, and your vows and your freewill offerings, and the firstlings of of your herds and of your flocks; And there ye shall eat before the Lord your God, and ye shall rejoice in all that ye put your hand unto, ye and your households, wherein the Lord thy God hath blessed thee. We are commanded to go into the house of the Lord. It is at the house of the Lord we hear the Word of God, we worship, we praises the Lord, give our tithes and offering and we meet sister and brother in the Lord, and new friends.

Acts 2:41-47 Then they that gladly received His word were baptized: and the same day there were added unto them about three thousand souls. And they continued stedfastly in the apostles' doctrine and fellowship, and in breaking of bread, and in prayers. And fear came upon every soul; and many wonders and signs were done by the apostles. And all that believed were together, and had all things common; and sold their possessions and goods, and parted them to all men, as every man had need. And they, continuing daily with one accord in the temple, and breaking bread from house to house, did eat their meat with gladness and singleness of heart. Praising God, and having favour with all the people. And the Lord added to the church daily such as should be saved. It is in the house of the Lord where we receive strength and encouragement. We can learn to talk to God in the house of the Lord.

The house of the Lord can be a place to hide from trouble. As we entrance into the house of the Lord we find comfort, and find answer to problem, and relieve from the care of his life. Psalm 27:4-6 One thing have I desired of the Lord, that will I seek after; that I may dwell in the house of the Lord all the days of my life, to behold the beauty of the Lord, and to enquire in His temple. For in the time of trouble He shall hide me in his pavilion:

in the secret of His tabernacle shall He hide me; He shall set me up upon a rock. And now shall mine head be lifted up above mine enemies round about me: therefore will I offer in his tabernacle sacrifices of joy; I will sing, yea, I will sing praises unto the Lord. Hear, O Lord, when I cry with my voice: have mercy also upon me and answer me.

House of the Lord will prevent us from backsliding. Psalm 73:1-17 Truly God is good to Israel, even to such as are of a clean heart. But as for me, my feet were almost gone; my steps had well nigh slipped. For I was envious at the foolish, when I saw the prosperity of the wicked. For there are no bands in their death: but their strength is firm. They are not in trouble as other men; neither are they plagued like other men. Therefore pride compasseth them about as a chain; violence covereth them as a garment. Their eyes stand out with fatness: they have more than heart could wish. They are corrupt, and speak wickedly concerning oppression: they speak loftily. They set their mouth against the heavens, and their tongue walketh through the earth. Therefore his people return hither: and waters of a full cup are wrung out to them. And they say, how doth God know? And is there knowledge in the most High? Behold, these are the ungodly, who proper in the world; they increase in riches; Verily I have cleansed my heart in vain, and washed my hands in innocency. For all the day long have I been plagued and chastened every morning. If I say, I will speak thus; behold, I should offend against the generation of thy children. When I thought to know this, it was too painful for me. Until I went into the sanctuary of God; then understood I their end.

We have been commanded not to forsaken the assembling of ourselves together. Hebrews 10:23-29 Let us hold fast the profession of our faith without wavering; (for He is faithful that promised :) And let us consider one another to provoke unto love and to good works: Not forsaking the assembling of ourselves together, as the manner of some is; but exhorting one another; and so much the more, as ye see the day approaching. For if we sin willfully after that we have received the knowledge of the truth, there remaineth no more sacrifice for sins, but a certain fearful looking for of judgment and fiery indignation, which shall devour the adversaries. He that despised Moses' law died without mercy under two or three witnesses: Of how much sorer punishment, suppose ye, shall he be thought worthy, who hath trodden under foot the Son of God, and hath counted the blood of the covenant, wherewith he was sanctified, an unholy thing, and hath done despite unto the Spirit of Grace?

We need to be planted in the house of the Lord. Psalm 92:12-15 The righteous shall flourish like the palm tree; He shall grow like a cedar in Lebanon. Those that be planted in the house of the Lord shall flourish in the courts of our God. They shall still bring forth fruit in old age; they shall be fat and flourishing; to shew that the Lord is upright: He is my rock, and there is no unrighteousness in Him.

In the body of Christ there is work for all of us to do. Never come into the body of Christ and just sit take parts and join in. Don't look down on yourself, just because you feel as someone is more talent than you are.

God has given you a gift use the gift God has given you for the body of Christ. You are important to the body of Christ. I Corinthians 12:18 But now hath God set the members every one of them in the body, as it hath pleased Him. Let God use you in His church.

There is no perfect church. We all are growing learning and been mature by the Lord. We are perfect through the blood of Jesus Christ. Therefore when you find a church, stay there if they are preaching the Word of God. Don't just run from church to church. Let the Lord clean you. He will mature you and make you Holy. Don't run from your problem. James1:2-5 My brethren, count it all joy when ye fall into divers temptations; Knowing this, that the trying of your faith worketh patience. But let patience have her perfect work, that ye may be perfect and entire, wanting nothing. If any of you lack wisdom, let him ask of God, that giveth to all men liberally, and upbraideth not; and it shall be given him.

I Corinthians 12:12 For by one Spirit are we all baptized into one body, whether we be Jews or Gentiles, whether we be bond or free; and have been all made to drink into one Spirit. For the body is not one member, but many. So allow God to use you do your part in the body of Christ whether you sing, dance, preach, minister, or take up the offering let God use you with the gift He has put within you.

When God want to use someone else be happy. Thank the Lord for the gift He has put within them. Philippians 2:2-4 Fulfill ye my joy, that ye be likeminded, having the same love, being of one accord, of one mind. Let nothing be done through strife or vainglory but in lowliness of mind let each esteems other better than themselves. Look not every man on his own things, but every man also on the things of others.

Allow the Lord to use you, your brethren, and your sister in Christ as it please Him. For we are all need for the body of Christ and have different gifts. I Corinthians 12:4-11 Now there are diversities of gifts, but the same Spirit. And there are differences of administrations, but the same

Lord. And there are diversities of operation, but it is the same God which worketh all in all. But the manifestation of the Spirit is given to every man to profit withal. For to one is given by the Spirit the word of wisdom; to another the word of knowledge by the same Spirit; to another faith by the same Spirit; to another the gifts of healing by the same Spirit; To another the working of miracles; to another prophecy; to another discerning of spirits; to another divers kinds of tongues; to another the interpretation of tongues. But all these worketh that one and the selfsame Spirit, dividing to every man severally as He will. Therefore we all have gift, so let God use us for His glory.

I Corinthians 12:18 But now hath God set the members every one of them in the body, as it hath pleased Him. Thank the Lord, He has chosen who will be the hand, foot eyes, and tongue. It is as it pleases the Lord. Not my will but it is His will and we are there to bring glory to the Lord. Every part of our body is necessary and contributes to our whole body.

I Corinthians 12:14-21 For the body is not one member, but many. If the foot shall say, because I am not the hand, I am not of the body, is it therefore not of the body? And if the ear shall say, because I am not the eye, I am not of the body; is it therefore not of the body? If the whole body were an eye, where where the hearing? If the whole were hearing, where was the smelling? But now hath God set the members every one of them in the body, as it hath pleased Him. And if they were all one member, where were the body? But now are they many members, yet but one body. And the eye cannot say unto the hand, I have no need of thee: nor again the head to the feet, I have no need of you. We need one another God has designed it that way. And I need the body of Christ more than the body of Christ needs me. We are all need.

I Corinthians 12:22-26 Nay, much more those members of the body, which seem to be more feeble, are necessary; And those members of the body, which we think to be less honourable, upon these we bestow more abundant honor; and our uncomely parts have more abundant comeliness. For our comely parts has no need: but God hath tempered the body together, having given more abundant honour to that part which lacked: That there should be no schism in the body; but that the members should have the same care one for another. And whether one member suffers, all the members suffer with it; or one member be honoured, all the members rejoice with it. Paul said the less honorable parts of the human body are important to the functions of the body. We don't see our heart, but without it there is no us. Our liver is very important to the function of the body. The liver breaks down waste matter in the blood and manufactures blood proteins. In our body, it is used to help clean out other organs, without the liver and heart we will not exist. We need one another that person that don't have much to say or do is important to the body of Christ upon these we show more abundant honour.

Ephesians 4:1-6 Therefore, the prisoner of the Lord, beseech you that ye walk worthy of the vocation wherewith ye are called. With all lowliness and meekness, with longsuffering, forbearing one another in love. Endeavouring to keep the unity of the Spirit in the bond of peace. There is one body, and one Spirit, even as ye are called in one hope of your calling. One Lord, one faith, one baptism. One God and Father of all, who is above all, and through all, and in you all. God want want to keep unity with unity there is nothing that we can't do if we have unity.

There is only one body and we are to be together in the body of Christ when the command was given to wait for the Holy Ghost they were together Acts 1:4 And, being assembled together with them, commanded them that they should not depart from Jerusalem, but wait for the promise of the Father, which, saith He, ye have heard of me.

On the day of Pentecost the saint were together and on one accord. Acts 2:1-4 And when the day of Pentecost was fully come, they were all with one accord in one place. And suddenly there came a sound from heaven as of a rushing mighty wind, and it filled all the house where they were sitting. And there appeared unto them cloven tongues like as of fire, and it sat upon each of them. And they were all filled with the Holy Ghost, and began to speak with other tongues, as the Spirit gave them utterance.

After the day of Pentecost the saint were together and had all things in common, Acts 2:41-44 Then they that gladly received His word were baptized; and the same day there were added unto them about three thousand souls. And they continued stedfastly in the apostle's doctrine and fellowship, and in breaking of bread, and in prayers. And fear came upon every soul: and many wonders and signs were done by the apostles. And all that believed were together, and had all things common.

God has saved us and made us alive through the Spirit. Ephesians 2:5 Even when we were dead in sins, hath quickened us together with Christ. (By grace ye are saved :) Ephesians 2:1 And you have he quickened who were dead in trespasses and sins.

Saint is raised up together. Ephesians 2:6 And hath raised us up together in Christ Jesus.

Saint has been made to sit together. Ephesians 2:6 And made us sit together in heavenly places in Christ Jesus. Jesus Christ sacrifice has broken down the middle wall of partition. Ephesians 2:13-16 But now in Christ Jesus ye who sometimes were far off are made nigh by the blood of Christ. For He is our peace, who hath made both one, and hath broken down the middle wall of partition between us. Having abolished in His flesh the enmity, even the law of commandments contained in ordinances; for to make in Himself of twain one new man, so making peace. And that he might reconcile both unto God in one body by the cross, having slain the enmity thereby.

Saint is building together. Ephesians 2:21-22 In whom all the building fitly framed together growth unto an holy temple in the Lord. In whom ye also are builded together for a habitation of God through the Spirit.

The saint is fitly together. Ephesians 4:16 From whom the whole body fitly joined together and compacted by that which every joint supplieth, according to the effectual working in the measure of every part, maketh increase of the body unto the edifying of itself in love.

Saint is knit together. Colossians 2:2 That their hearts might be comforted, being knit together in love, and unto all riches of the full assurance of understanding, to the acknowledgment of the mystery of God, and of the Father, and of Christ. Colossians 2:19 And not holding the head, from which all the body by joints and bands having nourishment ministered, and knit together, increaseth with the increase of God.

Saint strives together. Philippians 1:27 Only let your conversation be as it be as it becometh the gospel of Christ. That whether I come and see you, or else be absent, I may hear of your affairs, that ye stand fast in one Spirit, with one mind striving together for the faith of the gospel.

The body is tempered together. I Corinthians 12:21-24 And the eye cannot say unto the hand, I have no need of thee: nor again the head to the feet, I have no need of you. Nay, much more those members of the body, which seem to be more feeble, are necessary. And those members of the body, which we think to be less honourable, upon these we bestow more abundant honour; and our uncomely parts have more abundant comeliness. For our comely parts have no need; but God hath tempered the body together, having given more abundant honour to that part which lacked.

Saint is to live with Christ. I Thessalonians 5:10 Who dies for us, that, whether we wake or sleep, we should live together with Him.

Saint has been planted together in the likeness of Jesus death. Romans 6:5 For if we have been planted together in the likeness of His death, we shall be also in the likeness of His resurrection.

Saint is to be glorified together. Romans 8:16-17 The Spirit itself beareth witness with our spirit, that we are the children of God. And if children, then heirs, heirs of God and jointheirs with Christ; if so be that we suffer with him, that we may be also glorified together.

Saint will be caught up together. I Thessalonians 4:16-18 For the Lord Himself shall descend from heaven with a shout, with the voice of the archangel, and with the trump of God; and the dead in Christ shall rise first. Then we which are alive and remain shall be caught up together with them in in the clouds, to meet the Lord in the air: and so shall we ever be with the Lord. Wherefore comfort one another with these words.

Saint is to be comfort together. Romans 1:12 That is, that I may be comforted together with you by the mutual faith both of you and me.

YES, I CAN BE AN EFFECTIVE WITNESS. What is the best tool for winning the lost to Christ is a heart full of love and the Word of God.

Luke 19:9-10 And Jesus said unto him, This day is salvation come to this house, forsomuch as he also is a son of Abraham. For the Son of Man is come to seek and to save that which is lost. Jesus came to save and if winning soul was Jesus business we as saint should make it our business.

John 3:17-18 For God sent not His Son into the world to condemn the world; but that the world through him might be saved. He that believeth on Him is not condemned: but he that believeth not is condemned already, because he hath not believed in the name of the only begotten Son of God. God want people saved. Jesus died that we might have everlasting life. We are not to condemn but to let people know that Jesus dies for our sin and He is a deliverer.

Luke 12:8-9 Also I say unto you, Whosoever shall confess me before men, him shall the Son of man also confess before the angels of God. But he that denied me before the men shall be denied before the angels of God.

Winning the lost is the most important to Jesus. 2 Peter 3:8-9 But beloved, be not ignorant of this one thing, that one day is with the Lord as a thousand years, and a thousand years as one day. The Lord is not slack concerning his promise, as some men count slackness; but is longsuffering to us-ward, not willing that any should perish, but that all should come to repentance.

Witnessing is something that should never cease. Isaiah 62:6 I have set watchman upon thy walls, o Jerusalem, which shall never hold their peace day nor night: ye that make mention of the Lord, keep not silence.

Witness should take place in the home. Mark 5:18-19 And when he was come into the ship, he that had been possessed with the devil prayed him that He might be with Him. Howbeit Jesus suffered Him not, but saith unto him, Go home to thy friends, and tell them how great things the Lord hath done for thee, and hath had compassion on thee.

The Holy Ghost just doesn't help you witness but Holy Ghost make you a witness. You are witness. Just as a doctor is a doctor. You are a witness. Acts 1: 8 But ye shall receive power, after that the Holy Ghost is come upon you: and ye shall be witnesses unto me both in Jerusalem, and in all Judaea, and in Samaria, and unto the uttermost part of the earth. Isaiah 43:10 Ye are my witnesses, saith the Lord, and my servant whom I have chosen; that ye may know and believe me, and understand that I am He before me there was no God formed, neither shall there be after me.

Witness should be done without fear, and shame. 2 Timothy 1:7-8 For God hath not given us the spirit of fear; but of power, and of love, and of a sound mind. Be not thou therefore ashamed of the testimony of our Lord, nor of me His prisoner; but be thou partaker of the afflictions of the gospel according to the power of God.

Tell other about the Lord. Psalm 66:16 Come and hear, all ye that fear God, and I will declare what He hath done for my soul. Tell other how the Lord forgave you of all your sin and fill you with the Holy Ghost, and gave you peace. Just tell somebody about the Lord. John 4:4-29 And He must needs go through Samaria. Then cometh He to a city of Samaria, which is called Sychar, near to the parcel of ground that Jacob gave to his son Joseph. Now Jacob's well was there. Jesus therefore, being wearied with His journey, sat thus on the well: and it was about the sixth hour. There cometh a woman of Samaria to draw water: Jesus saith unto her, Give me to drink. (For His disciples were gone away unto the city to buy meat.) Then saith the woman of Samaria unto Him, How is it that thou, being a Jew, askest drink of me, which am a woman of Samaria? For the Jews have no dealings with the Samaritans. Jesus answered and said unto her. If thou knewest the gift of God, and who it is that saith to thee, Give me to drink; thou wouldest have asked of Him, and He would have given thee living water. The woman saith unto Him, Sir, thou hast nothing to draw with, and the well is deep: from whence then hast thou that living water? Art thou greater than our father Jacob, which gave us the well, and drank thereof himself, and his children, and his cattle? Jesus answered and said unto her, Whosoever drinketh of this water shall thirst again: But whosoever drinketh of this water that I shall give him shall never thirst; but the water that I shall give him shall be in him a well of water springing up into everlasting life. The woman saith unto Him, Sir, give me this water, that I thirst not, neither come hither to draw. Jesus saith unto her, Go, call thy husband, and come hither. The woman answered and said, I have no husband. Jesus unto her. Thou hast well said, I have no husband. For thou hast had five husbands; and he whom thou now hast is not thy husband; in that saidst thou truly. The woman saith unto him, Sir, I perceive that thou art a prophet. Our fathers worshipped in this mountain; and ye say, that in Jerusalem is the place where men ought to worship. Jesus saith unto her, Woman, believe me, the hour cometh, when ye shall neither in this mountain, nor yet at Jerusalem, worship the Father. Ye worship ye know not what: we know what we worship: for salvation is of the Jews. But the hour cometh and now is, when the true worshippers shall worship the Father in spirit and in truth: for the Father seeketh such to worship. God is a Spirit: and they that worship Him must worship him in spirit and in truth. The woman saith unto Him, I know that Messias cometh, which is called Christ: when He is come, He will tell us all things. Jesus saith unto her, I that speak unto thee am He. And upon this came His disciples, and marveled that He talked with the woman: yet no man said, what seekest thou or, Why talkest thou with her? The woman then left her waterpot, and went her way into the city, and saith to the men. Come; see a man, which told me all things that ever I did: is not this the Christ. Just go and tell someone about Jesus. Tell them that Jesus forgive, save, fill with the Holy Ghost, deliver, heals and He is everything we need and more.

Proverbs 11:30 The fruit of the righteous is a tree of life; and he that winneth souls is wise. To be an effective witness we need the Holy Ghost. For the Holy Ghost is what makes us a witness and makes us wise. Colossians 2:2-3 That their hearts might be comforted, being knit together in love, and unto all riches of the full assurance of understanding, to the acknowledgement of the mystery of God, and of the Father, and of Christ. In whom are hid all the treasures of wisdom and knowledge. All the wisdom, we need to witness is in Christ.

Present Jesus and not yourself. John 12:32 And I, if I be lifted up from the earth, will draw all men unto me.

Only God can draw a person. John 6:44 No man can come to me, except the Father which hath sent me draw him: and I will raise him up at the last day. So just sow the word of God and let God do the drawing. Our job is just to sow the Word of God. Mark 4:3-9 Hearken; Behold, there went out a sower to sow. And it came to pass, as he sowed, some fell by the way side, and the fowls of the air came and devoured it up. And some fell on stony ground, where it had not much earth; and immediately it sprang up, because it had no depth of earth: But when the sun was up, it was scorched: and because it had no root, it withered away. And some fell among thorns, and the thorns grew up, and choked it, and it yielded no fruit. And other fell on good ground, and did yield fruit that sprang up and increased; and brought forth, some thirty and some sixty and some a hundred. And He said unto them, He that hath ears to hear, let him hear. Our job is to sow the Word of God in love. Let God give the increase.

Never be jealous because someone wins more soul than you. Just let the Lord get the glory. I Corinthians 3:3-9 For ye are yet carnal: for whereas there is among you envying, and strife, and divisions, are ye not carnal, and walk as men? For while one saith, I am of Paul; and another, I am of Apollos; are ye not carnal? Who then is Paul, and who is Apollos; but ministers by whom ye believed, even as the Lord gave to every man? I have planted, Apollos watered; but God gave the increase. So then neither is he that planteth anything, neither he that watereth; but God that giveth the increase. Now he that planteth and he that watereth are one: and every man shall receive his own reward according to his own labour. For we are labourers together with God: ye are God's husbandry, ye are God's building.

Remember you have the Word of God. The Word of God is just what a person need. For the Word of God is God. John 1:1-2 In the beginning was the Word, And the Word was with God, and the Word was God. The same was in the beginning with God.

Always spend time in prayer. Jeremiah 33:3 Call unto me, and I will answer thee, and shew thee great and mighty things, which thou knowest not. He will prepare you. He will guide you. We only need to spent time with the Lord in prayer.

Study the Word of God. 2 Timothy 2:15 Study to shew thyself approved unto God, a workman that needeth not to be ashamed, rightly dividing the word of truth. We must study to feed ourselves and those we are witnessing to. Memorize scripture on salvation, repenting, water baptize, and the Holy Ghost.

Sometime you may have to deal with questions. When someone ask you a question and you didn't know the answer, and the Holy Ghost gave you the answer. Put the answer up somewhere you might need it again. You don't need to know the answer to every question because you have the One who can answer every problem.

Everyone should be a prospect. Acts 22:15 For thou shalt be witness unto all men of what thou hast seen and heard.

When the Holy Ghost laid someone on your heart doesn't delay in going to talk to that person. Hebrews 3:7-8 Wherefore (as the Holy Ghost saith, Today if ye will hear His voice, Harden not your hearts, as in the provocation, in the day of temptation in the wilderness.

Yes, I can obey my pastor. What is a pastor? Your pastor is the one that teach you the word of God and the one that the Lord has made your overseer. You need a pastor. Jeremiah 10:23 O Lord, I know that the way of man is not in himself: it is not in man that walketh to direct his step. The Lord will direct you through your pastor. Ezekiel 3:17-21 Son of man, I have made thee a watchman unto the house of Israel: therefore hear the word at my mouth; and give them warning from me. When I say unto the wicked, Thou shalt surely die, and thou givest him not warning, nor speakest to warn the wicked from his wicked way, to save his life; the same wicked man shall die in his iniquity; but his blood will I require at thine hand. Yet if thou warn the wicked and he turn not from his wickedness, nor from his way, he shall die in his iniquity; but thou hast delivered thy soul. Again, when a righteous man doth turn from his righteousness, and commit iniquity, and I lay a stumbling block before him, he shall die: because thou hast not given him warning, he shall die in his sin, and his righteousness which he hath done shall not be remembered; but his blood will I require at thine hand. Nevertheless if thou if thou warn the righteous man, that the righteous sin not, and he doth not sin, he shall surely live, because he is warned; also thou hast delivered thy soul.

Your pastor is a gift from God. Your pastor and other ministries will help you come into perfection. Ephesians 4:8-14 Wherefore he saith, when he ascended up on high, he led captivity captive, and gave gifts unto men. (Now that He ascended, what is it but that He also descended first into the lower parts of the earth? He that descended is the same also that ascended up far above all heavens, that He might fill all things.) And He gave some, apostles; and some, prophets; and some, evangelists; and some, pastors and teachers; for the perfecting of the saints, for the work of the ministry, for the edifying of the body of Christ. Till we all come in the unity of the faith, and of the knowledge of the Son of God, unto a perfect man, unto the measure of the stature of the fullness of Christ. That we henceforth be no more children, tossed to and fro, and carried about with every wind of doctrine, by the sleight of men, and cunning craftiness, whereby they lie in wait to deceive.

Your pastor will help take your children out of the snare of the devil. 2 Timothy 2:24-26 And the servant of the Lord must not strive; but be gentle unto all men, apt to teach, patient. In meekness instructing those that oppose themselves; if God peradventure will give them repentance to the acknowledging of the truth; And that they may recover themselves out of the snare of the devil, who are taken captive by him at his will.

Your pastor is the one who will feed you and your family the word of God. Acts 20:28 Take heed therefore unto yourselves, and to all the flock, over the which the Holy Ghost hath made you overseers, to feed the church of God, which He hath purchased with His own blood. For I know this, that after my departing shall grievous wolves enter in among you, not sparing the flock. Also of your own selves shall men arise, speaking perverse things, to draw away disciples after them. Therefore watch and remember that by the space of three years I ceased not to warn every one might and day with tear. Your pastor and other ministries will protect you from the wolves. I Peter 5:1-4 The elders which are among you I exhort, who am also an elder, and a witness of the sufferings of Christ, and also a partaker of the glory that shall be revealed. Feed the flock of God which is among you, taking the oversight thereof, not by constraint, but willingly; not for filthy lucre, but of a ready mind. Neither as being lords over God's heritage, but being ensamples to the flock. And when the chief Shepherd shall appear, ye shall receive a crown of glory that fadeth not away. The deacon is not the one that runs the church. The pastor is the overseer.

God will use your pastor to save other and build faith. I Corinthians 1:21 For after that in the wisdom of God the world by wisdom knew not God, it pleased God by the foolishness of preaching to save them that believe. Romans 10:13-17 For whosoever shall call upon the name of the Lord shall be saved. How then shall they call on Him in whom they have not believed? And how shall they believe in Him of whom they have not heard? And How shall they hear without a preacher? And how shall they preach, except they be sent? As it is written, how beautiful are the feet of them that preach the gospel of peace and bring glad tidings of good things! But they have not all obeyed the gospel. For Esaias saith, Lord, who hath believed our report? So then faith cometh by hearing, and hearing by the Word of God.

Your pastor is your leader. Hebrews 13:7 Remember them which have the rule over you, who have spoken unto you the Word of God: whose faith follow, considering the end of their conversation.

Your pastor is the watchmen for your soul. Hebrews 13:17 Obey them that have the rule over you, and submit yourselves: for they watch for your souls, as they that must give account, that they may do it with joy, and not with grief: for that is unprofitable for you.

Your pastor has responsibilities to you and you have responsibilities to your pastor.

We are to obey the pastor. As long as the pastor asks you to do what is right and scripture, you are to obey your pastor. Hebrew 13:17 Obey them that have the rule over you, and submit yourselves: for they watch for your souls, as they that must give account, that they may do it with joy, and not with grief: for that is unprofitable for you.

We are to remember our pastor. Hebrews 13:7 Remember them which have the rule over you, who have spoken unto you the word of God: whose faith follow, considering the end of their conversation.

We are to salute our pastor. Hebrews 13:24 Salute all them that have the rule over you, and all the saints. They of Italy salute you.

We are to esteem our pastor very highly. I Thessalonians 5:13 And to esteem them very highly in love for their work's sake. And be at peace among yourselves.

We are to count our pastor worthy of double honour. I Timothy 5:17 Let the elders that rule well be counted worthy of double honour especially they who labour in the word and doctrine. Exodus 33:8 And it came to pass, when Moses went out unto the tabernacle, that all the people rose up, and stood every man at his tent door, and looked after Moses, until he was gone into the tabernacle. Acts 28:10 Who also honoured us with many honours; and when we departed, they laded us with such things as were necessary. Philippians 2:29 Receive him therefore in the Lord with all gladness; and hold such in reputation.

Do not accept an accusation against your pastor except before two or three witnesses. I Timothy 5:19-20 Against an elder receive not an accusation, but before two or three witnesses. Them that sin rebuke before all, that others also may fear. I Timothy 5:1 Rebuke not an elder, but intreat him as a father; and the younger men as brethren. We are not to rebuke our pastor; we are to allow those that are over them to rebuke them. I Timothy 4:14 Neglect not the gift that is in thee, which was given thee by prophecy, with the laying on of the hands of the presbytery. The presbytery was a group of elder and if there was problem with any pastor or other elder. They were turn over to the presbytery. The saint of God did not judge the elders. Therefore to stay out of trouble with God does not accuse or accept an accusation on your pastor. Numbers 12:1-16 And Miriam and Aaron spake against Moses because of the Ethiopian woman whom he had married: for he had married an Ethiopian woman. And they said, hath the Lord indeed spoken only by Moses? Hath he not spoken also by us? And the Lord heard it. (Now the man Moses was very meek, above all the men which were upon the face of the earth.) And the Lord spake suddenly unto Moses, and unto Aaron, and unto Miriam, Come out ye three unto the tabernacle of the congregation, and they they came out. And the Lord came down in the pillar of the cloud, and stood in the door of the tabernacle, and called Aaron and Miriam and they both came forth. And He said, hear now my words: If there be a prophet among you, I the Lord will make myself known unto him in a vision, and will speak unto him in a dream. My servant Moses is not so, who is faithful in all mine house. With him will I speak mouth to mouth, even apparently, and not in dark speeches, and the similitude of the Lord shall he behold: wherefore then were ye not afraid to speak against my servant Moses? And the anger of the Lord was kindled against them; and he departed. And the cloud departed from off the tabernacle; and, behold, Miriam became leprous, white as snow: and Aaron looked upon Miriam, and, behold, she was leprous. And Aaron said unto Moses, Alas, my lord, I beseech thee;

lay not the sin upon us, wherein we have done foolishly, and wherein we have sinned. Let her not be as one dead, of whom the flesh is half consumed when he cometh out of his mother's womb. And Moses cried unto the Lord, saying, Heal her now, O God, I beseech thee. And the Lord said unto Moses, if her father had but spit in her face, should she not be ashamed seven days? Let her be shut out from the camp seven days, and after that let her be received in again. And Miriam was shut out from the camp seven days: and the people journeyed not till Miriam was brought in again. And afterward the people removed from Hazeroth, and pitched in the wilderness of Paran. Do not speak against the man of God.

Do not muzzle your pastor. I Timothy 5:18 For the scripture saith, Thou shalt not muzzle the ox that treadeth out the corn. And the labor is worthy of his reward. It was against the law for the ox to work and be not able to eat of the corn. I Corinthians 9:14 Even so hath the Lord ordained that they which preach the gospel should live of the gospel. In the dispensation of promise the man of God received the tithes. Genesis 14:18-20 And Melchizedek King of Salem brought forth bread and wine: and He was the priest of the most High God. And he blessed him, and said, blessed be Abram of the most high God, possessor of heaven and earth: And blessed be the most high God, which hath delivered thine enemies into thy hand. And he gave him tithes of all.

What are tithes?

Genesis 14:20 And blessed be the most high God, which hath delivered thine enemies into thy hand. And he gave him tithes of all. Hebrews 7:1-4 For this Melchisedec, King of Salem, priest of the most high God, who met Abraham returning from the slaughter of the kings, and blessed him; To whom also Abraham gave a tenth part of all; first being by interpretation King of righteousness, and after that also King of Salem, which is King of peace; Without father, without mother, without descent, having neither beginning of days, nor end of life; but made like unto the Son of God; abideth a priest continually. Now consider how great this man was, unto whom even the patriarch Abraham gave the tenth of the spoils. Therefore tithe is the tenth of our income but tithe is more than a tenth of our income, tithe is the first tenth of our income. Matthew 6:33 But seek ye first the kingdom of God, and His righteousness; and all these things shall be added unto you. Always put the Lord first.

Dekatos mean tenth, which is a Greek word.

Maasrah mean tenth, which is a Hebrew word.

Tithes took place before the law, first mention of tithes in Genesis 14:20 And blessed be the most high God, which hath delivered thine enemies into thy hand. And he gave him tithes of all. Abraham gave tithes under the dispensation of promise. The dispensation of promise took place 430 Year before the dispensation of the law. Galatians 3:16-19 Now to Abraham and his seed were the promises made. He saith not, and to seeds, as of many; but as of one, and to thy seed, which is Christ. And this I say, the covenant, that was confirmed before of God in Christ, the law, which was four hundred and thirty years after, cannot disannul, that it should make the promise of none effect. For if the inheritance be of the law, it is no more of promise: but God gave it to Abraham by promise. Wherefore then serveth the law? It was added because of transgressions, till the seed should come to whom the promise was made; and it was ordained by angels in the hand of a mediator. Genesis 28:20-22 And Jacob vowed a vow, saying if God will be with me, and will keep me in this way that I go, and will give me bread to eat, and raiment to put on. So that I come again to my father's house in peace: then shall the Lord be my God. And this stone, which I have set for a pillar, shall be God's house: and of all that thou shalt give me I will surely give the tenth unto thee. Jacob gave tithe under the dispensation of promise and Abraham gave tithes under the dispensation of promise. The Bible say if we are the seed of Abraham then do the work of Abraham.

Tithe is Holy. Leviticus 27:30-34 And all the tithe of the land, whether of the seed of the land, or of the fruit of the tree, is the Lord's holy unto the Lord. And if a man will at all redeem aught of his tithes, he shall add therewith the fifth part thereof. And concerning the tithe of the herd, or of the flock, even of whatsoever passeth under the rod, the tenth shall be holy unto the Lord. He shall not search whether it be good or bad, neither shall he change it: and if he change it at all, then both it and the change thereof shall be holy: it shall not be redeemed. These are the commandments, which the Lord commanded Moses for the children of Israel in Mount Sinai. Under the law if you didn't give your tithe when you were so to (redeem it) you add a fifth part or 20%. If you get behind in your tithes do you need to add 20% that between you and God and your pastor. My advice gives your tithes when you are supposed to and you won't have that problem.

Tithe is an investment Matthew 6:19-20 Lay not up for yourselves treasures upon earth, where moth, and rust doth corrupt, and where thieves break through and steal: But lay up for yourselves treasures in heaven, where neither moth nor rust doth corrupt, and where thieves do not break through nor steal: Luke 6:38 Give and it shall be given unto you; good measure, pressed down, and shaken together, and running over, shall men give into your bosom. For with the same measure that ye mete withal it shall be measured to you again.

Tithe is a blessing. Malachi 3:10 Bring ye all the tithes into the storehouse, that there may be meat in mine house, and prove me now herewith, saith the Lord of Hosts, if I will not open you the windows of heaven, and pour you out a blessing, that there shall not be room enough to receive it. Galatians 3:9 So then they which be of faith are blessed with faithful Abraham.

Tithe is a law. Deuteronomy 12:6 And Thither ye shall bring your burnt offerings, and your sacrifices, and your tithes, and heave offerings of your hand, and your vows, and your freewill offerings, and the firstlings of your herds and of your flocks. Deuteronomy 14:22 Thou shall truly tithe all the increase of thy seed, that the field bringeth forth year by year.

Tithe is a teacher. Deuteronomy 14:22-23 Thou shalt truly tithe all the increase of thy seed, that the field bringeth forth year by year. And thou shalt eat before the Lord thy God, in the place which he shall choose to place His name there, the tithes of thy corn, of thy wine, and of thine herbs, an of thy flocks; that thou mayest learn to fear the Lord thy God always.

Tithe is to be brought to the house of the Lord. Tithe is not to be given anywhere tithe is to be brought to the house of the Lord. Malachi 3:10 Bring ye all the tithes into the storehouse, that there may be meat in mine house, and prove me now herewith, saith the Lord of Hosts, if I will not open you the windows of heaven, and pour out a blessing; that there shall not be room enough to receive it.

Tithe is a way of destroy the power of enemy in our life. John 10:10 The thief cometh not, but for to steal, and to kill, and to destroy: I am come that they might have life, and that they might have it more abundantly. There is a thief, a destroyer, and a killer in our life but tithing break the power of the enemy. Malachi 3:11-12 And I will rebuke the devourer for your sakes, and he shall not destroy the fruits of your ground; neither shall your vine cast her fruit before the time in the field, saith the Lord of Hosts. And all nations shall call you blessed: for ye shall be a delightsome land, saith the Lord of Hosts

Tithe is a way of honouring the Lord. Proverbs 3:9-10 Honour the Lord with thy substance, with the firstfruits of all thine increase: So shall thy barns be filled with plenty, and thy presses shall burst out with new wine.

Tithing is worship. Tithing is a time of worship. It should never be a time of regretting but a time of rejoicing. 2 Corinthians 9:7 For God loveth a cheerful giver. Deuteronomy 26:1-11 And it shall be, when thou art come in unto the land which the Lord thy God giveth thee for an inheritance, and possesses it, and dwellest therein; That thou shalt take of the first of all the fruit of the earth, which thou shalt bring of thy land that the Lord thy God giveth thee, and shalt put it in a basket, and shalt go unto the place which the Lord thy God shall choose to place His name there. And thou shalt go unto the priest that shall be in those days, and say unto him, I profess this day unto the Lord thy God, that I am come unto the country which the Lord sware unto our fathers for to give us. And the priest shall take the basket out of thine hand, and set it down before the altar of the Lord thy God. And thou shalt speak and say before the Lord thy God, A Syrian ready to perish was my father, and he went down into Egypt, and sojourned there with a few, and became there a nation, great, mighty, and populous; And the Egyptians evil entreated us, and afflicted us, and laid upon us hard bondage: And when we cried unto the Lord God of our fathers, the Lord heard our voice, and looked on our affliction, and our labour, and our oppression: And the Lord brought us forth out of Egypt with a mighty hand, and with an outstretch arm, and with great terribleness, and with signs, and with wonders: And he hath brought us into this place, and hath given us this land, even a land that floweth with milk and honey. And now, behold, I have brought the firstfruits of the land, which thou, O Lord, hast given me. And thou shalt set it before the Lord thy God, and worship before the Lord thy God: And thou shalt rejoice in every good thing which the Lord thy God hath given unto thee, and unto thine house, thou, and the Levite, and the stranger that is among you.

Tithe should be used to support the Levites. Tithing was first give to Melchisedec Genesis 14:19-20 And he blessed him, and said, Blessed be Abram of the most high God, possessor of heaven and earth: And blessed be the most High God, which hath delivered thine enemies into thy hand. And he gave him tithes of all. Abraham gave tithe to Melchisedec. Our priesthood which is Christ was order after Melchisedec. Hebrews 5:1-11 For every high priest taken from among men is ordained for men in things pertaining to God, that he may offer both gifts and sacrifices for sins; Who can have compassion on the ignorant, and on them that are out of the way, for that he himself also is compassed with infirmity. And by reason hereof he ought, as for the people so also for himself, to offer for sins. And no man taketh this honour unto himself but he that is called of God, as was Aaron. So also Christ glorified not Himself to be made a high priest; but He that said unto Him, Thou art my son, today have I begotten thee. As He saith also in another place, Thou art a priest for ever after the order of Melchisedec. Who in the days of His flesh, when He had offered up prayers and supplications with strong crying and tears unto Him that was able to save Him from death, and was heard in that he feared: Though he was a Son, yet learned he obedience by the things which he suffered; And being made perfect, he became the author of eternal salvation unto all them that obey Him, Called of God an high priest after the order of Melchisedec. Of whom we have many things to say and hard to be uttered, seeing ye are dull of hearing. Levite received tithe for taking care of the tabernacle and offer sacrifices. Numbers 18: 20-24 And the Lord spake unto Aaron, Thou shalt have no inheritance in their land, neither shalt thou have any part among them: I am thy part and thine inheritance among the children of Israel. And, behold, I have given the children of Levi all the tenth in Israel for an inheritance, for their service which they serve, even the service of the tabernacle of the congregation. Neither must the children of Israel henceforth come nigh the tabernacle of the congregation, lest they bear sin, and die. But the Levites shall do the service of the tabernacle of the congregation, and they shall bear their iniquity: it shall be a statute forever throughout your generations, that among the children of Israel they have no inheritance. But the tithes of the children of Israel, which they offer as a heave offering unto the Lord, I have given to the Levites to inherit: therefore I have said unto them. Among the children of Israel they shall have no inheritance. Even though Paul was a tentmaker, the church also help supported Him. I Corinthians 9:1-14 Am I not an apostle? Am I not free? Have I not seen Jesus Christ our Lord? Are not ye my work in the Lord? If I be not an apostle unto others, yet doubtless I am to you: for the seal of mine apostleship are ye in the Lord. Mine answer to them that do examine me is this. Have we not power to eat and drink? Have we not power to lead about a sister, a wife, as well as other apostles, and as the brethren of the Lord, and Cephas? Or I only and Barnabas, have not we power to forbear working? Who goeth a warfare any time at his own charges? Who planteth a vineyard, and eateth not of the fruit therof? Or who feedeth a flock, and eateth not of the milk of the flock? Say I these things as a man? Or saith not the law the same also? For it is written in the Law of Moses, Thou shalt not muzzle the ox that treadeth out the corn. Doth God take care for oxen? Or saith He it altogether for our sakes? For our sakes, no doubt this is written: that he that ploweth should plow in hope; and that he that thresheth in hope should be partaker of his hope. If we have sown unto you spiritual things, is it a great thing if we shall reap your carnal things. If others be partakers of this power over you, are not we rather? Nevertheless we have not used this power; but suffer all things, lest we should hinder the gospel of Christ. Do ye not know that they which minister about holy things live of the things of the temple? And they which wait at the altar are partakers with the altar? Even so hath the Lord ordained that they which preach the gospel should live of the gospel?

Should tithes be used to support widows and orphans? There are at least eight requirements for a widow in order for the church to take care of them financially. I Timothy 5:1-16 Rebuke not an elder, but intreat him as a father; and the younger men as brethren; the elder women as mothers; the younger as sisters, with all purity. Honour widows that are widows indeed. But if any widow has children or nephews, let them learn first to shew piety at home, and to requite their parents: for that is good and acceptable before God. Now she that is a widow indeed, and desolate, trusteth in

God, and continueth in supplications and prayers night and day. But she that liveth in pleasure is dead while she liveth. And these things give in charge, that they may be blameless. But if any provide not for his own, and specially for those of his own house, he hath denied the faith, and is worse than an infidel. Let not a widow be taken into the number under threescore years old, having been the wife of one man. Well reported of for good works; if she has brought up children, if she has lodged strangers, if she has washed the saints' feet, if she has relieved the afflicted, if she has diligently followed every good work. But the younger widows refuse: for when they have begun to wax wanton against Christ, they will marry: Having damnation, because they have cast off their first faith. And withal they learn to be idle, wandering about from house to house, and not only idle, but tattlers also and busybodies, speaking things which they ought not. I will therefore that the younger women marry, bear children, guide the house, give none occasion to the adversary to speak reproachfully. For some are already turned aside after Satan. If any man or woman that believeth has widows, let them relieve them, and let not the church be charged; that it may relieve them that are widows indeed. Widows need to meet the eight requirements and also if they have children or nephew, they are to take care of the widow that the church will not be charged.

Should the pastor give tithe? Numbers 18:26-32 Thus speak unto the Levites, and say unto them. When ye take of the children of Israel the tithes which I have given you from them for your inheritance, then ye shall offer up a heave offering of it for the Lord, even a tenth part of the tithe. And this your heave offering shall be reckoned unto you, as though it were the corn of the threshing floor, and as the fullness of the winepress. Thus ye also shall offer a heave offering unto the Lord of all your tithes, which ye receive of the children of Israel; and ye shall give thereof the

Lord's heave offering to Aaron the priest. Out of all your gifts ye shall offer every heave offering of the Lord, of all the best thereof, even the hallowed part thereof out of it. Therefore thou shalt say unto them, When ye have heaved the best thereof from it, then it shall be counted unto the Levites as the increase of the threshingfloor, and as the increase of the winepress. And ye shall eat it in every place; ye and your households: for it is your reward for your service in the tabernacle of the congregation. And ye shall bear no sin by reason of it, when ye heaved from it the best of it: neither shall ye pollute the holy things of the children of Israel, lest ye die. The children of Israel gave tithe to the Levite; Levite gave tithes to the Priest. The saints are to give tithes to the pastor, pastor is to give tithes to the one that is over him or he is to put tithes back into the church.

When we give our tithe and offering we cause blessing upon our house. Ezekiel 44:30 And the first of all the firstfruits of all things, and every oblation of all, of every sort of your oblations shall be the priest's ye shall also give the priest the first of your dough, that he may cause the blessing to rest in thine house.

What happen if we refuse to give tithes? We become robbers Malachi 3:8-10 Will a man robs God? Yet ye have robbed me. But ye say, Wherein have we robbed thee? In tithes and offerings. Ye are cursed with a curse: for ye have robbed me, even this whole nation. Bring ye all the tithes into the storehouse, that there may be meat in mine house, and prove me now herewith, saith the Lord off hosts, if I will not open you the windows of heaven, and pour you out a blessing, that there shall not be room enough to receive it. When we don't give our tithes and offering, we don't allow God to prove Himself to us. You hinder the hand of God from working in your life. The windows of heaven are closed to us. We put money in a bag with holes in it. We are always losing our income. Haggai 1:1-10 In the second year of Darius the king, in the sixth month, in the first day of the month, came the word of the Lord by Haggai the prophet unto Zerubbabel the son of Shealtiel, governor of Judah, and to Joshua the son of Josedech, the high priest, saying. Thus speaketh the Lord of hosts, saying, this people say, the time is not come, the time that the Lord's house should be built. Then came the Word of the Lord by Haggai the prophet, saying Is it time for you, O ye, to dwell in your ceiled houses, and this house lie waste? Now therefore thus saith the Lord of hosts; consider your ways. Ye have sown much, and bring in little; ye eat, but ye have not enough; ye drink, but ye are not filled with drink; ye clothe you, but there is none warm, and he that earneth wages earneth wages to put it into a bag with holes. Thus saith the Lord of hosts. Consider your ways. Go up to the mountain, and bring wood, and build the house; and I will take pleasure in it, and I will be glorified saith the Lord. Ye looked for much, and lo, it came too little; and when ye brought it home, I did blow upon it. Why? Saith the Lord of host, Because of mine house that is waste, and ye run every man unto his own house. Therefore the heaven over you is stayed from dew, and the earth is stayed from her fruit. Take care of the house of God, and God will take care of you.

Tithe is a covenant between you and God. When you give your tithe you said to God, I am putting you first in my life and you take care of me and all of my bills. Genesis 28:20-22 And Jacob vowed a vow, saying, If God will be with me, and will keep me in this way that I go, and will give me bread to eat, and raiment to put on. So that I come again to my father's house in peace; then shall the Lord be my God: And this stone, which I have set for a pillar, shall be God's house: and of all that thou shalt give me I will surely give the tenth unto thee.

Tithes is the ten of our income and offering should be given as the Lord has prosperous us I Corinthians 16:1-2 Now concerning the collection for the saints, as I have given order to the churches of Galatia, even so do ye. Upon the first day of the week let every one of you lay by him in store, as God hath prospered him, that there be no gatherings when I come.

Offering are to be given according to what we have. 2 Corinthians 8:12-15 For if there be first a willing mind, it is accepted according to that a man hath, and not according to that he hath not. For I mean not that other men be eased, and ye burdened: But by an equality, that now at this time your abundance may be a supply for their want, that their abundance also may be a supply for your want: that there may be equality: As it is written, he that had gathered much had nothing over; and he that had gathered little had not lack.

We are to give offering in the way we want to receive, if you want a little blessing give a little but if you want a big blessing you might want to empty out. 2 Corinthians 9:6 But this I say, he which soweth sparingly shall reap also sparingly; and he which soweth bountifully shall reap also bountifully.

We are to give offering as we purpose in our heart. 2 Corinthians 9:7 Every man according as he purposeth in his heart, so let him give; not grudgingly, or of necessity: for God loveth a cheerful giver.

We are to give with simplicity. Romans 12:8 Or he that exhorteth, on exhortation: he that giveth, let him do it with simplicity; he that ruleth, with diligence; he that sheweth mercy, with cheerfulness.

Always honour your pastor and God will honour you. The Bible says the elder that ruleth well should get double honour especially they who labour in the word and doctrine. If you don't give tithe and offering you are not giving double honour.

The pastor responsibility is to take heed to his self. Acts 20:28 Take heed therefore unto yourselves, and to all the flock, over the which the Holy Ghost hath make you overseers, to feed the church of God, which He hath purchased with His own blood. A pastor cannot give to you what he doesn't possess. If the pastor is weak, He will have weak followers, if he is strong in the Lord, his followers will be strong in the Lord. If your pastor is carnally you will be carnally. If your pastor is spiritually, you can become spiritually. A pastor cannot give to you what he doesn't possess. His first calling was not called to be a pastor his first calling is to be a saint to live a holy and sanctified life.

The pastor is to feed the saint of God. I Peter 5:1-4 The elders which are among you I exhort, who am also an elder, and a witness of the sufferings of Christ, and also a partaker of the glory that shall be revealed: feed the flock of God which is among you, taking the oversight thereof, not by constraint, but willingly; not for filthy lucre, but of a ready mind; Neither as being lords over God's heritage, but being ensamples to the flock. And when the chief Shepherd shall appear, ye shall receive a crown of glory that fadeth not away. John 21:15-19 So when they had dines, Jesus saith to Simon Peter, Simon, son of Jonas, lovest thou me more than these? He saith unto him, Yea, Lord; thou knowest that I love thee. He saith unto him. Feed my lambs. He saith to him again the second time, Simon, son of Jonas, lovest thou me? He saith unto him, Yea, Lord; thou knowest that I love thee. He saith unto him, Feed my sheep. He saith unto him the third time, Simon, son of Jonas, lovest thou me? Peter was grieved because He said unto him the third time, Lovest thou me? And he said unto Him, Lord, thou knowest all things; thou knowest that I love thee. Jesus saith unto him, Feed my sheep. Verily, verily, I say unto thee, when thou wast young, thou girdedst thyself, and walkedst whither thou wouldest: but when thou shalt be old, thou shalt stretch forth thy hands, and another shall gird thee, and carry thee whither thou wouldest not. This spake he, signifying by what death he should glorify God. And when he had spoken this, he saith unto him, follow me. A good pastor follows Jesus and is willing to lay his life down for the sheep. He will protect them make sure they get a well balance diet. He will make sure the word of God is rightly divided for the sheep. He will allow nothing poison to enter into their belly. Jeremiah 3:15 And I will give you pastors according to mine heart, which shall feed you with knowledge and understanding. Jeremiah 23:4 And I will setup shepherds over them which shall feed them: and they shall fear no more, nor be dismayed, neither shall they be lacking, saith the Lord. The pastor that God put over you, if you listen and obey will cause fear to leave, dismay and lack disappear.

Pastor is to reprove, rebuke, and exhort. 2 Timothy 4:2-4 Preach the word; be instant in season, out of season; reprove (show them their fault), rebuke (take a strong dislike to sin in their life), and exhort (encourage them to continue to do right) with all longsuffering and doctrine. For the time will come when they will not endure sound doctrine; but after their own lusts shall they heap to themselves teachers, having itching ears; And they shall turn away their ears from the truth, and shall be turned unto fables.

Pastor is to preach the word of God. 2 Timothy 4:2 Preach the word; be instant in season, out of season; a pastor is call above all thing to preach the word of God for this is the avenue God have choose to save men by. I Corinthians 1:21 For after that in the wisdom of God the world by wisdom knew not God, it pleased God by the foolishness of preaching to save them that believe. Romans 10:13-15 For whosoever shall call upon the name of the Lord shall be saved. How then shall they call on Him in whom they have not believed? And how shall they believe in Him of whom they have not heard? And how shall they hear without a preacher? And how shall they preach, except they be sent? As it is written, How beautiful are the feet of them that preach the gospel of peace, and bring glad tidings of good things!

Pastor is to teach the word of God. The Bible talk more about teach than the Bible talk about preach. The word of God must be plain and applicable to everyday life. 2 Timothy 2:24 And the servant of the Lord must not strive; but be gentle unto all men, apt to teach, patient. I Timothy 4:11 These things command and teach.

Pastor is a watchman of our soul. Ezekiel 33:17 Son of man, I have made thee a watchman unto the house of Israel: therefore hear the word at my mouth, and give them warning from me. When I say unto the wicked, Thou shalt surely die, and thou givest him not warning, nor speakest to warn the wicked from his wicked way, to save his life;; the same wicked man shall die in his iniquity; but his blood will I require at thine hand.

Pastor is to make disciples, baptize, and teach the saint to observe all things the Lord has commanded. Matthew 28:17-20 And when they saw Him, they worshipped Him: but some doubted. And Jesus came and spake unto them, saying, all power is given unto me in heaven and in earth. Go ye therefore, and teach all nations, baptizing them in the name of the Father, and of the Son, and of the Holy Ghost: Teaching them to observe all things whatsoever I have commanded you: and lo, I am with you always, even unto the end of the world. Amen. Acts 8:26-39 And the angel of the Lord spake unto Phillip, saying, Arise, and go toward the South unto the way that goeth down from Jerusalem unto Gaza, which is desert. And he arose and went: and, behold, a man of Ethiopia, an eunuch of great authority under Candace queen of the Ethiopians, who had the charge of all her treasure, and had come to Jerusalem for to worship, Was returning, and sitting in his chariot read Esaias the prophet. Then the Spirit said unto Phillip, Go near and join thyself to this chariot. And Phillip ran thither to Him and heard him read the prophet Esaias, and said, Understandest thou what thou readest? And he said, how can I, except some man should guide me? And he desired Phillip that he would come up and sit with him. The place of the scripture which he read was this, He was led as a sheep to the slaughter; and like a lamb dumb before his shearer, so opened, he not His mouth: In His humiliation his judgment was taken away: and who shall declare his generation? For his life is taken from the earth. And the eunuch answered Philip, and said, I pray thee, of whom speaketh the prophet this? Of himself, or of some other man? Then Phillip opened his mouth, and began at the same scripture, and preached unto him Jesus. And as they went on their way, they came unto a certain water: and the eunuch said, See, here is water; what doth hinder me to be baptized? And Phillip said, If thou believest with all thine heart, thou mayest. And he answered and said, I believe that Jesus Christ is the Son of God. And he commanded the chariot to stand still: and they went down both into the water, both Phillip and the eunuch; and he baptized him. And when they were come up out of the water, the Spirit of the Lord caught away Phillip, and the eunuch saw him no more: and he went on his way rejoicing.

Pastor is to equip the saints for the work of the ministry. Ministry means to serve. We often speak of the ministry as the fivefold ministry. Every saint is called to minister to usher, clean the church, or the ministry of giving. Too often we leave work for the pastor that need to be carried out by other saint therefore the pastor can equip us for minster. The pastor needs to spend time in prayer and in studying of the word and not in motoring the church yard. The pastor is to equip the saint for the work of the ministry that they may be able to do the work of the minister. Acts 6:1-4 And in those days, when the number of the disciples was multiplied, there arose a murmuring of the Grecians against the Hebrews, because their widows were neglected in the daily ministration. Then the twelve called the multitude of the disciples unto them, and said, it is not reason that we should leave the word of God, and serve tables. Wherefore, brethren, look ye out among you seven men of honest report, full of the Holy Ghost and wisdom, whom we may appoint over this business. But we will give ourselves continually to prayer, and to the ministry of the word.

Pastor is to edify the church. The word edify mean to construct, to strengthen to improve morally or spiritually. Edify mean to build up. Ephesians 2:20-21 And are built upon the foundation of the apostles and prophets, Jesus Christ himself being the chief corner stone; In whom all the building fitly framed together growth unto an holy temple in the Lord. The pastor is an encourager, an exhorter, and an edifier for the body of Christ.

Your Pastor is the one that is like a savior for the saint. 2 Corinthians 2:16 To the one we are the savour of death unto death; and to the other the savour of life unto life. And who is sufficient for these things?

Promises for the believer: I Kings 8:56 Blessed the Lord, that hath given rest unto His people Israel, according to all that He promised: there hath not failed one word of all His good promise, which He promised by the hand of Moses His servant. Romans 4:21 And being fully persuaded, that what He had promised, He was able to perform. 2 Corinthians 1:20 For all the promises of God in Him are yea, and in Him. Amen, unto the glory of God by us.

Promises to the afflicted. Psalm 34:19 Many of the afflictions of the righteous: but the Lord delivereth him out of them all.

Psalm 30:5 For His anger endureth but a moment; in His favour is life: weeping may endure for a night, but joy cometh in the morning.

Psalm 41:3 The Lord will strengthen him upon the bed of languishing: thou wilt make all his bed in his sickness.

Isaiah 43:2 When thou passest through the waters, I will be with thee; and through the rivers, they shall not overflow thee: when thou walkest through the fire, thou shalt not be burned; neither shall the flame kindle upon thee.

Romans 8:28 And we know that all things work together for good to them that love God, to them who are the called according to his purpose.

2 Corinthians 4:17 For our light affliction which is but for a moment, worketh for us a far more exceeding and eternal weight of glory.

Revelation 21:4 And God shall wipe away all tears from their eyes; and there shall be no more death, neither sorrow, nor crying neither shall there be any more pain: for the former things are passed away.

Psalm 37:4 Trust in the Lord, and do good, so shalt thou dwell in the land, and verily thou shalt be fed.

Mark 9:23 Jesus said unto him, If thou canst believe, all things are possible to him that believeth.

Luke 17:8 And the Lord said, if ye had faith as a grain of mustard seed, ye might say unto this sycamine tree, be thou plucked up by the root, and be thou planted in the sea; and it should obey you

Mark 11:22-24 And Jesus answering saith unto them, Have faith in God. For verily I say unto you, That whosoever shall say unto this mountain, Be thou removed, and be thou cast into the sea; and shall not doubt in his heart, but shall believe that those things which he saith shall come to pass; he shall have whatsoever he saith. Therefore I say unto you, what things soever ye desire, when ye pray, believe that ye receive them, and ye shall have them.

John 1:12 But as many as received him, to them gave he power to become the sons of God, even to them that believe on His name.

John 6:35 And Jesus said unto the, I am the bread of life: he that cometh to me shall never hunger, and he that believeth on me shall never thirst.

Promise to the humble Psalm 138:6 Though the Lord be high, yet hath he respect unto the lowly: but the proud he knoweth afar off.

Luke 14:11 For whosoever exalteth himself shall be abased: And he that humbleth himself shall be exalted.